Augsburg Commentary on the New Testament

JAMES
R. A. Martin

I-II PETER / JUDE
John H. Elliott

Augsburg Publishing House
Minneapolis, Minnesota

AUGSBURG COMMENTARY ON
THE NEW TESTAMENT

JAMES, 1-2 PETER, JUDE

Copyright © 1982 Augsburg Publishing House

Library of Congress Catalog Card No. 82-70962

International Standard Book No. 0-8066-1937-6

Scripture quotations unless otherwise noted are from the Revised Standard Version of the Bible, copyright 1946, 1952, and 1971 by the Division of Christian Education of the National Council of Churches.

Manufactured in the United States of America

Contents

FOREWORD

The AUGSBURG COMMENTARY ON THE NEW TES-
TAMENT is written for laypeople, students, and pastors. Laypeople will use it as a resource for Bible study at home and at
church. Students and instructors will read it to probe the basic
message of the books of the New Testament. And pastors will
find it to be a valuable aid for sermon and lesson preparation.

The plan of each Commentary is designed to enhance its
usefulness. The Introduction presents a topical overview of the
biblical book to be discussed and provides information on the
historical circumstances in which that book was written. It
may also contain a summary of the biblical writer's thought.
In the body of the Commentary, the interpreter sets forth in
brief compass the meaning of the biblical text. The procedure
is to explain the text section by section. Care has also been
taken to avoid scholarly jargon and the heavy use of technical
terms. Because the readers of the Commentary will have their
Bibles at hand, the biblical text itself has not been printed
out. In general, the editors recommend the use of the Revised
Standard Version of the Bible.

The authors of this Commentary Series are professors at
seminaries and universities and are themselves ordained clergy-
persons. They have been selected both because of their exper-
tise and because they worship in the same congregations as the
people for whom they are writing. In elucidating the text of

Scripture, therefore, they attest to their belief that central to the faith and life of the church of God is the word of God.

The Editorial Committee

Roy A. Harrisville
Luther-Northwestern Seminaries
St. Paul, Minnesota

Jack Dean Kingsbury
Union Theological Seminary
Richmond, Virginia

Gerhard A. Krodel
Lutheran Theological Seminary
Gettysburg, Pennsylvania

JAMES

R.A. Martin

INTRODUCTION

James has had a stormy and uncertain history in the Christian church. It had a difficult time getting into the New Testament canon, achieving canonical status in the Greek church in the fourth century, the Latin church in the fifth century, and the Syrian church only in the eighth century. The Roman Catholic Council of Trent (1546), which officially fixed many post-Reformation Roman Catholic doctrines, listed James among the deutero-canonical writings of the New Testament, that is, those that were accepted only gradually by the church. Luther's judgment on it as "an epistle of straw" is often quoted. He took this position because it does not clearly teach salvation by grace. His somewhat more favorable comment later, however, in the preface to his commentary on James should also be noted: "I think highly of James and regard it as valuable, although it was rejected in early days. . . . I do not consider it to be apostolic." Luther would consider only those New Testament writings apostolic which clearly and explicitly preach Jesus Christ and the salvation which is found in him.

1. Literary Form

The title given to this writing in the earliest Greek manuscripts (ca A.D. 350) is "The Epistle of James." The only indication in the book itself that it is an epistle or letter is the first verse, which follows the form of the salutations characteristic of Greek letters in the first Christian century. Further, study of the contents of James reveals that most of the usual marks of an actual letter are absent, such as specific situations being addressed, news, personal messages, greetings, and a conclusion.

James is not, then, an actual letter to a specific person, church, or group of churches. Rather it is a series of loosely-connected moral and ethical admonitions and instructions. Other writings from this same general period suggest that James is best designated as a letter of exhortation or homily.

2. Author

In the first verse the author is designated as "James, a slave of God and of the Lord Jesus Christ." James is a very common Jewish and Christian name, used of no less than five individuals in the New Testament:

1. James, the father of Judas (not Iscariot), one of the twelve disciples (Luke 6:16)
2. James, the son of Alphaeus, also one of the twelve disciples (Luke 6:15)
3. James the younger, mentioned in Mark 15:40
4. James, the brother of John, one of the sons of Zebedee, and a member of an apparent inner circle of the twelve disciples (Mark 3:17)
5. James, the brother of Jesus (Mark 6:3)

Nothing is known of the first three in this list. The fourth entry—James, the son of Zebedee—was the first of the twelve disciples to be martyred, beheaded by Herod Agrippa in A.D. 44 (Acts 12:2). It is improbable that any of these four can be the James referred to in the salutation to this epistle.

The last name on the list, James, the brother of Jesus, has frequently been posited as the author, though the first reference to him as the writer of this letter is rather late—by the church father Origen in the third century.

James, the Lord's brother, was evidently not a disciple during Jesus' ministry (cf. Mark 3:31-35 and John 7:5); but, as the early church tradition in 1 Corinthians 15:1-7 indicates, the resurrected Jesus appeared to him and in connection with this experience he may have converted. Paul (Gal. 1-2) and the book of Acts (12:17; 15:13-21; 21:17, 18) further indicate that this James very early became the leader of the Christian church in Jerusalem, probably from about A.D. 40 until his martyrdom in 62.

It is, however, improbable that James, the brother of Jesus and leader of the Jewish Christian church in Jerusalem, wrote this letter. Some of the weightier reasons for this opinion are as follows:

1. It is strange that the author nowhere designates himself as the Lord's brother, nor does he make any references to the life and ministry of Jesus.

2. The language used has features characteristic of polished and literary Greek. It is improbable that the brother of Jesus and leader of the conservative Aramaic-speaking Jewish Christian church in Jerusalem would have had command of such a high level of Greek style and usage. Acts 6:1–8:3 is generally understood to refer to the separation of the Greek-speaking element of the church from the community in Jerusalem.

3. The ideas in the epistle and its relationship to Paul's ministry are best understood if James was written after Paul's ministry was completed—in the last decade or two of the first Christian century—and addresses a misunderstanding of Pauline teaching concerning faith and works.

For these reasons and others it is improbable that James, the brother of Jesus, was the author of this writing. At the same time there are features of the style and contents of the letter that indicate that the writer was making use of traditional material which goes back to the Palestinian, Aramaic-speaking period of the church, i.e., the period before the destruction of Jerusalem in A.D. 70.

First of all, many of the ideas in the letter are very Jewish—so Jewish that some have even suggested James was originally not a Christian letter at all, but a Jewish writing taken over with few changes by a later Jewish Christian author (cf. for example, its emphasis on prayer, almsgiving, ethical rules, etc.). Further, while the Greek is in many ways polished and literary, it is also in some respects very strongly influenced by the Semitic languages—Hebrew and Aramaic (cf. "James, Epistle of" in the Supplementary Volume of *The Interpreter's Dictionary of the Bible*).

The most probable explanation for this strangely mixed Jewish/Christian, good Greek/Semitized Greek character of James is that it was written by a Hellenistic Christian of the Jewish Christian, non-Pauline church outside Palestine some time toward the end of the first Christian century, making use of some earlier traditional Palestinian material. As a literary device this author put the name **James** in the salutation of the letter, thereby indicating either that the origin of much of the tradition was in the Jerusalem church or that, in his opinion, some of the material went back to James, the leader of the Jerusalem church.

3. Audience

The churches addressed would seem to be those in the diaspora (Syria, Asia Minor, and Europe) in which the Jewish element had remained strong. Not only was this true of the church in Jerusalem, but there is evidence throughout the empire of non-Pauline, Jewish-oriented Christian communities, which were loyal to the early church in Jerusalem and less than enthusiastic about some of the developments in the Pauline mission.

4. James and Paul

The relationship of the letter of James to Paul and his letters and ideas has been variously interpreted. There are those, largely on the basis of the James 2:14-26, who have felt that James is consciously arguing against Paul. This does not seem likely. As Dibelius concludes:

> The connections between James and the letter of Paul ought not at the outset be overrated. For though the sections in Jas. 2:14-26 seems to presuppose an acquaintance with definite Pauline slogans, it also demonstrates precisely the fact that any penetrating reading of the letters of Paul upon the part of James is out of the question. . . . All things considered, one can say that James obviously writes after Paul, but that he is not writing under the sort of Pauline influence which could be explained as resulting from the reading of Paul's letters (*James*, pp. 29f.).

The position adopted in this commentary is that James is not reacting directly against Paul or his letters, but rather against a misunderstood Paulinism which has appeared among those to whom he writes.

5. Purpose

The writer, then, is a Christian, writing to other Christians, using traditional teaching material. He reflects a deep concern for the moral quality of life of those who, in Christ, share in the new age and anticipate its culmination at his return.

The writer does not intend to present the totality of Christian truth, but rather seeks to motivate and guide Christian people to live their faith. As such James has much that parallels the sayings of Jesus in the Synoptic Gospels and the exhortation sections in the last half of most of Paul's letters.

As Kümmel has correctly noted, James' "indispensable task in the canon can only be achieved where someone as a Christian has already heard the message of Jesus or of Paul, and through James has his vision sharpened for the exhortation to the work which grows out of faith . . ." (*Introduction to the New Testament*, p. 416).

OUTLINE OF JAMES

Because James is basically parenesis (i.e., advice, counsel, or exhortation) one should not expect to find clear continuity of thought. It is of the very nature of parenesis to lack such continuity and be characterized by superficial, catch-word connections and recurring motifs. With that qualification, the following outline of the contents of James will be followed in the commentary:

I. Salutation (1:1)

II. Miscellaneous Admonitions concerning Trials and Temptations (1:2-18)
   A. The Value of Trials (1:2-4)
   B. The Admonition to Seek Understanding (1:5-8)
   C. Poverty and Riches (1:9-11)
   D. God's Role in Trials (1:12-18)

III. Admonition concerning Hearing and Doing the Word (1:19-27)
   A. The Importance of Hearing (1:19-21)
   B. The Importance of Hearing That Results in Action (1:22-25)
   C. The Importance of the Right Kind of Action (1:26-27)

IV. Warning Against Partiality (2:1-13)

15

SELECTED BIBLIOGRAPHY

M. Dibelius, *James* rev. by H. Greeven and transl. by M. A. Williams in *Hermeneia* ed. by H. Koester, Philadelphia: Fortress, 1976. This is and will be for years to come the standard English commentary on the Greek text of James.

Older, but still useful commentaries on the Greek Text

J. H. Ropes, *A Critical and Exegetical Commentary on the Epistle of St. James* in *International Critical Commentary*. Edinburgh: Clark, 1916.

C. L. Mitton, *The Epistle of James*. Grand Rapids: Eerdmans, 1966.

Commentaries on the English Text (arranged chronologically with more recent titles first)

Sidebottom, E. M. *James, Jude and 2 Peter* in *The Century Bible*. London: Nelson, 1967.

Reicke, B., *The Epistles of James, Peter, and Jude* in *Anchor Bible*. New York: Doubleday, 1964.

Barclay, W., *The Letters of James and Peter* in the *Daily Study Bible*. Philadelphia: Westminster, 1960.

Blackman, E. C., *The Epistle of James* in *Torch Bible Commentaries*. Naperville: Allenson, 1957.

Easton, B. S., "The Epistle of James" in *The Interpreter's Bible*. New York: Abingdon, 1957.

Tasker, R. V. G., *The General Epistle of James* in *The Tyndale New Testament Commentaries*. London: Tyndale, 1956.

Moffatt, James, *The General Epistles*. London: Hodder and Stoughton, 1928.

COMMENTARY

■ Salutation (1:1)

James—The name here does not indicate the writer of the epistle (cf. Introduction). The use of this name is, rather, a literary device to indicate the author's awareness that much of the traditional material used in writing this book had its origin in the early Palestinian Jewish-Christian church. Some of the material in this epistle may indeed have come from James, the brother of Jesus, who was the leader of the Jerusalem church from ca. A.D. 40 to his martyrdom in 62. The actual author of the book is unknown.

servant—a more accurate translation of the Greek (*doulos*) would be "slave." This is a positive theological concept for many of the New Testament writers, emphasizing the commitment, obedience, and loyalty that marks their relationship to God who has manifested himself in their Lord and Savior Jesus Christ.

the twelve tribes—This phrase can be understood in a number of ways. It can refer to the Jews as a nation. Some scholars have seen in this phrase an indication that originally this letter or part of it was a Jewish document. More probable is the view that this is a way of referring to the Christian church as the new people of God, the New Israel.

19

in the Dispersion—Dispersion is a technical term for those Jews who lived outside of Palestine, scattered among the nations. Here it most probably refers to Jewish Christians throughout Syria, Asia Minor and Europe; but it could also have metaphorical reference to all Christians away from their true home, heaven (cf. also 1 Peter 1:1).

Greeting—This is the usual form of Greek salutations. It differs from the Jewish "peace" and distinctly Christian "grace" of the salutations in Paul's letters (e.g., Rom. 1:7; 1 Thess. 1:1).

■ Miscellaneous Admonitions Concerning Trials and Temptations (1:2-18)

The material in this section is loosely connected, but not unrelated. The first part (vv 2-8) colors the meaning of the entire group (vv 2-18). It appears to be made up of four or five separate units, depending on whether v 12 is considered as an independent beatitude concerning endurance or is to be taken intimately with vv 13-18:

A. The Value of Trials (vv 2-4)

B. The Admonition to Seek Understanding Concerning Trials (vv 5-8)

C. Poverty and Riches (vv 9-11)

D. God's Role in Trials (vv 12-18)

The Value of Trials (1:2-4)

Three aspects of these verses need comment.

trials (v 2)—The Greek word for trial has two related but different meanings. It means both "test" and "temptation." In a test, the tester hopes and intends that the tested person successfully passes the test; in a temptation, the tempter intends that the tempted one fail and succumb. In the Bible only the context can make clear which meaning the writer intends. While God tests us, he never tempts us. A little later in this chapter (vv 13, 14) the writer deals with this distinction and the theological implications involved. Here the writer means test, which will be successfully passed with beneficial results.

Count it all joy (v 2)—The theme of rejoicing in time of testing is frequent in the New Testament (cf. for example the Beatitudes, Matt. 5:10-12, and 1 Peter 1:6). This admonition is not pollyannish nor does it foster a martyr complex which derives unnatural satisfaction from suffering. The joy to be found in divine testing is indicated in vv 3 and 4—joy in the growth it brings: **steadfastness** (v 3) and wholeness (v 4), even as rigorous training enables an athlete to win the contest and the prize.

meet (v 2)—This word literally means "fall into" and implies that tests are not sought, but neither are they to be avoided at all costs when they confront us. If responded to properly such divine testing can draw us closer to God, enable us to experience his upholding power and give us stronger faith, greater maturity, and wholeness of character.

The Admonition to Seek Understanding (1:5-8)

At first glance these verses may seem unrelated to the previous section. However, since they are sandwiched in between sections on trials (vv 2-4) and temptations (vv 9-18), it is clear that in the writer's mind he means divine help, wisdom and understanding are needed to view testing in this way and so to benefit from it. The source of wisdom for Jewish people is God (cf. Prov. 9:10; Job 28:28) and wisdom must be sought from God by prayer.

Prayer is a favorite topic of James, one to which the writer returns a number of times (cf. 4:1-3 and 5:13-18). In this brief section he touches on three aspects of prayer: a) what to ask for—**wisdom**, especially wisdom concerning the role and value of the divine testing; b) how God feels about our asking—his eagerness for us to ask and the impartial generosity of his response to our asking (v 5); and c) how we are to feel about asking—certain of God's care and concern (vv 6-8).

with no doubting (v 6)—This phrase does not mean certainty on our part of *how* God will answer prayer, but only that he *will* surely answer. It is certainty concerning the nature and love of God, not certainty of our understanding God's plans and specific ways of dealing with us. Because we know and trust *him*, we can accept what he sends or allows even when we cannot understand. Thus we cannot dictate in prayer *what* he must do; only that he must be concerned and care.

Poverty and Riches (1:9-11)

In this section the writer contrasts the lot in life of the poor and the rich. These are favorite motifs of James, recurring in Chapters 2, 4 and 5.

It will be seen that the judgment of James on the rich is quite harsh, while the poor and powerless are viewed much more positively (similarly also Jesus in the Gospels—cf. for example Luke 6:20-26; 12:13-21; 16:19-25; Matt. 6:24-33). There is an implicit qualification operating here. The rich who come in for condemnation are those who draw a sense of security from their wealth and who use their position and power for selfish ends. The rich are not all like that, of course; but in the writer's mind the vast majority are, and the temptation to such false security is always there for those who have wealth and power.

So also when he speaks of the poor and helpless, the writer has in mind those who in their poverty and need turn to God in trust and humility. Again this is not necessarily the case. The writer would not praise the irreligious poor any more than he would castigate the wealthy who live lives of dependence on God and concern for other people.

In the light of the expectation of the return of Christ expressed in 5:7ff., it is probable that the author envisions the reversals mentioned in these verses as occurring at least then, if not earlier.

God's Role in Trials (1:12-18)

The little beatitude in v 12 points back to v 9 and particularly vv 2-4, indicating the blessed result of testing met in the right way. It provides a transition to the next verses (13-18) by reintroducing the word **trial,** taken there in its other and negative sense as temptation. These verses on temptation are brought up because of the two-fold meaning of trial. A theological misunderstanding of God and his dealings with people could result if this term is not carefully defined. But James clearly shows the true source of temptation (in vv 13-15) and states unambiguously God's constant goodness and concern. In this way the author excludes in the sharpest possible manner any thought that God can be conceived of as tempting people to sin. Rather, as James makes very clear in v 18, God only and always seeks to make us over into new beings, conformable to his own nature and perfection.

While v 17 is worded very obscurely in the Greek original, the main point of the verse is clear: God is unchangeable and his constancy is a constancy of goodness and love.

■ Admonition Concerning Hearing and Doing the Word (1:19-27)

The final verses of this section (vv 26-27) govern the thought of the entire unit which is concerned with the nature of truly religious persons and their relationship to God and to God's self-revelation in his Word.

The first part (vv 19-21) emphasizes openness to God's Word; the next section (vv 22-25) emphasizes obedience to that heard Word, for real hearing implies action. The final verses (vv 26-27), in language reminiscent of the prophets and the Gospels, show what truly religious activity growing out of the Word consists of.

The Importance of Hearing (1:19-21)

These verses contrast natural human tendencies and the effective power of God and his Word; therefore there is a need for a constant readiness to turn to that Word in openness to it and its power (v 19).

the implanted word (v 21) may be an allusion to baptism, a reminder of the nearness of that powerful Word in one's life. It can also be a reminder that the Word must be nurtured and that all hindering influences must be rooted out, if that Word is to be an effective power for everyday living.

The Importance of Hearing That Results in Action (1:22-25)

In this section James emphasizes what all know instinctively to be true—our lives are affected by what we hear and believe. Hearing has a special meaning in Jewish writings and involves commitment and obedience to what is heard. James reminds his readers of this.

In v 22, James is not contrasting a doer and a hearer; rather he contrasts two kinds of hearers—those who do something about what they hear and those who do not. This parallels very closely what James says later (2:24) about works and faith.

In vv 23-24, James indicates by a striking analogy the unnaturalness of hearing that does not result in appropriate action —this is as unnatural and foolish as going to a mirror to see how you look and then not making the necessary changes that the mirror clearly indicates. Rather (v 25) benefit comes when one acts in accordance with what one sees in the mirror.

the perfect law, the law of liberty needs some comment. One of the Jewish marks of this letter is the positive evaluation of law. It is frequent in the Old Testament (particularly the Psalms) and in Rabbinic writings—for example, Ps. 19:7

"The law of the Lord is perfect" and Aboth 6:2 "No man is free except the one who labors in the law."

The law is not the tyrannical force we Christians often consider it to be. Even Paul writes: "So the law is holy, and the commandment is holy and just and good. . . . We know that the law is spiritual. . . ." Rom 7:12, 14 (cf. also Gal. 6:2; 1 Cor. 9:21; Rom. 6:12-22). The law expresses the will of God. We have been created by him and it is life in conformity to our Maker's will that is found to be satisfying, liberating from all false slaveries, indeed, as James says, **blessed** (v 25).

The Importance of the Right Kind of Action (1:26-27)

The truly religious person is a person who acts, as well as hears and believes; but in these verses, James pushes the thought a bit farther. It is not just action itself, but the right kind of action that is important. Three kinds of action are specifically noted by James as being distinctly religious: 1) control of what we say; 2) care and concern for the weak, helpless, and disenfranchised; and 3) resistance to evil.

Religion involves self-control; new life in Christ is power for self-control. For James the tongue, what we say, is particularly difficult to control, as he suggested already in 1:19 and as he elaborates in 3:1-12. Religion, if it is true, is able to help even here, to change our daily lives, including what we say and how we speak to one another (v 25).

But more, true religion is particularly characterized by care and concern for the weak, the helpless, and the disenfranchised. How like the prophets (Micah 6:6-8; Isa. 1:10-17; Amos 5:21-24; Zech. 7:4-10; Hosea 6:6) and how like Jesus (Matt. 25:31-45; Mark 12:33, 40; Luke 10:25-37)! Not outward religiosity and formal rituals of worship, but care and concern for people in need—these are the marks of the truly religious person, who has experienced the grace, forgiveness, and care of God in Jesus Christ.

And finally (v 26b) such a religious person, one who has

been made new in Christ, will resist the evil and the evil influences in the world. For James, as for Paul (Gal. 5) and John (Chap 17), **world** is a negative concept (cf. James 4:4 also). It is life and culture as it is controlled or influenced by the forces of evil. It is God's good creation in the control of God's enemy. It is the world for which Christ died and which sought to destroy him. James does not here mean a piety which in pride and condemnation stands aloof from its environment but rather a piety which is involved in the world but does not succumb to the evil that God seeks to eradicate. James here says what Paul says in Rom. 12:2: "Do not be conformed to this world but be transformed by the renewal of your mind, that you may prove what is the will of God, what is good and acceptable and perfect."

■ Warning Against Partiality (2:1-13)

While it is true that there is no clear continuity of thought throughout James, the sections are often loosely related to one another.

These first verses of Chapter 2 have some contacts with what has just been discussed and with what will follow in 2:14-26. The last verses of Chapter 1 ended on a note of care and concern for God's poor and helpless ones; partiality toward the rich (the subject of these verses) is the other side of the coin. So also 2:14-26 speak of the importance of faith showing itself in a certain quality of life (2:18) and these verses (2:1-13 specify very clearly one of the qualities true faith should produce.

The unit itself (2:1-13) has a clearer structure than some of the earlier units. In 2:1 the author states his thesis, his basic admonition. In 2:2-4 he gives an example of such partiality that is condemned, and shows in 2:5-7 how this partiality disagrees with both God's own attitude (v 5) and common sense (vv 6-7). James 2:8-11 demonstrates the sinfulness and law-lessness of such partiality with a final warning (2:12-13) concerning the basis on which such lawlessness will be judged.

partiality (v 1) in the context clearly means treating those who have power, status, influence, and money with more respect than those who do not, in hopes of security, favor, and benefits.

faith of our Lord, as 2:14ff. shows, means "trust in Christ," not "belief in a body of doctrine." Reliance on the power and care and protection of Jesus is denied if we seek the security obtained by currying the favor of the powerful and influential of this world.

The next section 2:2-4 raises a number of issues. What is the meaning of **assembly?** The Greek word is *synagōgē* (synagogue) the term for the place of assembly for Jews (and Christians in the earliest period of the church) not *ekklēsia,* the word used for distinctly Christian worshiping groups. This may be an indication of traditional material from a much earlier period (before A.D. 70).

Further, what is the status of this person of power (v 2)? Is he a member of the Christian community or an outsider? The text does not make this clear. Later on (v 7) the rich person seems to be an outsider, but even there the interpretation is ambiguous.

Such partiality toward the powerful is wrong on two counts (2:5-7). It is the opposite of God's judgment (v 5), and their own daily experience warns them what kind of treatment can be expected from the rich (vv 6-7).

The phrase, **blaspheme that honorable name by which you are called** (v 7), requires comment. Blaspheming the name could refer to unbelievers abusing Christians and Christ himself. But would they then come to the Christian assembly as this illustration pictures them? Or does this refer to wealthy Christians who, by their unconcern for the poor and helpless, blaspheme the religion of Jesus Christ? Certainly this latter view would fit well with what James has to say about faith in 2:14-26.

In 2:8-11, the writer makes use of the Jewish doctrine of the complete unity of the law, so that a violation of one aspect or command thereby involves the breaking of the entire law (v 10). Paul reflects this same line of argumentation in Galatians 5:3 and 3:10b. James seems to mean that the command against partiality in Leviticus 19:15 is intimately connected with the love command in Leviticus 19:18. He wants the readers to realize that partiality is not a minor, isolated infraction, but has the same implications and results as a violation of the other commandments which they consider central and serious.

Therefore he gives the sharp warning in v 13: **For judgment is without mercy to one who has shown no mercy.** This statement is clearly reminiscent of those passages in the Gospels where Jesus warns his followers that God will withdraw his forgiveness from those who do not respond by forgiving others (Matt. 5:7; 7:1-2; Luke 6:37-38; Matt. 18:32-34; 6:14-15; Mark 11:25).

The final phrase in v 13 is a tremendous statement of the promise and power of God's grace. His mercy and forgiveness can change us into merciful and forgiving people. James wants his readers to take seriously the power of the Gospel as an agent for change in their lives. That is his concern also in the next section.

■ The Kind of Faith That Counts (2:14-26)

These verses are among the most misunderstood passages in the New Testament. One misconception is that James is here contrasting faith and works. This is not so. A careful reading of this passage (cf. v 18 especially) will reveal that James is actually contrasting *two types of faith*, only one of which is really faith at all.

Another misconception is that in this passage James teaches

a way of salvation that contradicts the way of salvation taught in the rest of the New Testament, particularly in Paul's letters. Again this is not so. There certainly is a difference in the way various New Testament writers talk about faith and about the life faith produces. But as will be shown in the interpretation of these verses, James is emphasizing a truth about faith which is not infrequently stated in the Gospels and which corresponds in *content,* and sometimes also in *wording,* with what Paul teaches in his letters.

Finally, most English translations of v 26 are misleading, including the RSV. This will be discussed in detail in the explanation of the verse below.

This passage is correctly divided in the RSV into two paragraphs. Verses 14-17 make the point that a faith worthy of the name produces results corresponding to its claim. In the next section vv 18-26 James contrasts *living* faith with *dead* "faith," and indicates the latter is no faith at all and cannot save anyone.

Dead Faith (2:14-17)

It is important to notice what James actually says here. In v 14 he does not say, "If a man *has* faith. . . ."; James rather says, **If a man *says* he has faith. . . .** James is talking about what a person claims or professes, and he points out that one's claims may or may not correspond to reality.

James is not concerned here with the nature of faith, whether it is true or false, orthodox and heretical. He is rather concerned with the difference between *the claim* to have faith and *actually having* faith.

In the RSV the last half of this verse reads: **Can his faith save him?** The Greek text reads: "Can *the* faith save him?" The article *the* in Greek is used to refer back to what has just been mentioned. In this case it refers back to **says he has faith** and really means: "Can *such* faith save him?" Can faith which is only claimed save a person? For James the clear answer is,

"Of course not!" In Greek there are ways to ask a question to show whether the questioner expects yes or no for an answer. James has the form which clearly indicates he expects the answer, "No." In English also we can make this clear by rewording the question: "Such faith is not able to save him, is it?" Clearly the expected answer is: "No, of course not."

In vv 15 and 16 James uses a comparison to drive home his point. This comparison is drawn from daily life and shows that what one professes does not always correspond to reality; that which is claimed does not always represent how the person actually feels.

James pictures a man who sees someone in need of food and clothing. This man says nice words to the needy person: **Go in peace, be warmed and filled,** or in other words: "I care about you." But he does not actually share any of his possessions with the needy person. Does such a person care? Of course not! If people care about the needy, they will share as best they can and try to help the sufferers meet their real needs. If people aren't willing to share what they have, they don't really care for those who are in need. The profession of concern is just that—mere profession, empty words—no real concern, only a *professed* concern; to be real, concern must have some evidence in concrete actions corresponding to the claim. Then James (v 17) makes the application: this is true about faith also. If people claim to have faith but give no evidence of that faith in the way they live, it is not real faith at all, but merely a claimed or professed faith, which James calls a dead faith (v 17). It is a faith that is not even worthy of the name.

Two Types of Faith (2:18-26)

In this section, James seeks in a variety of ways to convince those who think they need only to profess their faith that such a merely professed faith is no faith at all, that it does not meet the deepest spiritual needs, nor does it result in salvation.

James' line of argumentation is as follows. In v 18 he raises the question: How can you know whether faith is really present? Verse 19 shows that real faith is not intellectual assent to a proposition about God, but rather involves trust in that God. Then in vv 20-25, using examples drawn from the Old Testament, James demonstrates that faith and works (which are evidences of faith and grow out of it) are inseparable—two sides of the same coin. In the final verse of this section, James shows by another analogy that faith without works is no faith at all.

In v 18 James adopts a very graphic style of argumentation similar to the diatribe style employed by Jewish and Greek writers in the ancient world; that is, he sets up an imaginary conversation to dispute the point of the person who tries to separate faith and works. The imaginary opponent claims that he himself has faith and also seems to claim that James is only concerned about works. James, however, sets his opponent straight on both points: Show me the reality of your faith without works; and I will show the reality of my faith by the works it produces.

This is the key verse. James makes it absolutely clear that it is not a dispute over faith or works. It is, rather, a dispute over *two types of faith,* one of which claims to exist independently of works, the other producing works which demonstrate its validity. James' sentiments are with the latter: "I will show you my faith by my works." Nothing James says in the following verses is to be read in contradiction to what he explicitly states here. For him works are not a substitute for faith, but are the evidence of faith.

In v 19 James presents a deep insight into the nature of faith. It is not mere intellectual assent to a proposition about God and his nature. "God is one" was the central claim of the Jewish faith and basic to Christianity as well. Acknowledgment of this correct doctrine, however, is not in itself faith. Faith is trust in God. Even the evil beings (demons) acknowledge the nature and reality of God but they have neither fellowship with him nor trust in him.

The implication of this verse is that real faith will result in the trust, commitment, and obedience which correspond to that faith. This James will now illustrate with the examples of Abraham and Rahab.

James introduces a new example in v 20 for this merely professed faith which is really no faith at all. It is **barren** or useless. The picture is similar to that of "no profit" or "no benefit" mentioned earlier in 2:14-17. The image is of a tree barren of fruit and thus of no value and recalls comparisons Jesus makes in the Gospels (see for example Matt. 7:17-20).

Verses 21-24 bring forward, as demonstration of this claim, the figure of Abraham. While James here makes use of the very same verse of Genesis (15:6) that Paul uses in Romans 4:3, he does so in a quite different manner and for a quite different purpose.

In Romans 4 and Galatians 3 Paul demonstrates that Torah observance and circumcision have nothing to do with Abraham's status with God, since the Torah was given 430 years later through Moses (Gen. 3:17) and circumcision was instituted (Gen. 17) after God had already established his covenant with Abraham (Rom. 4:9-12).

James, on the other hand, is not discussing the role of either Torah or circumcision in bringing a person into a right relation to God. Rather, as will be shown below, he is reminding those who claim such a faith-relation to God that faith is inseparably bound up with the fruits, the results of that faith (James 2:22). Abraham demonstrated this kind of faith in God by his willingness to offer Isaac in obedience to God's will as it had been made clear to him (v 21).

Notice again, James does not speak of works as separate from faith; he does not speak of being justified by works alone—but rather he speaks of faith that **was active along with his works,** and faith that **was completed by works** (v 22).

He means they are inseparable, two sides of the same coin. The word **completed** should not be misunderstood here. James is not talking about one form of faith that is better than another. He is talking about whether faith is present at all. The coin is not complete unless it has two sides—heads and tails. And faith is not complete unless it produces works that grow out of this new relationship of trust. Thus, James says (v 23) that it is not surprising that the Scriptures declare Abraham righteous on the basis of his faith—his faith was obvious, demonstrated by his trust and obedience. It is clear, James continues (v 24), that a person is **justified by works** (which faith produces) **and not by faith alone** (not by that lip-service, nonproductive faith which is really no faith at all). This statement must be interpreted in the light of all James has said up to this point (vv 14, 17, 18, 22). It is the removal of v 24 from its connection with James' entire argument in vv 14-24 that has resulted in the false contradiction many have found between Paul and James.

It should also be noted that when James speaks about works and faith, he repeats the line of argument he used earlier in 1:22 about doing and hearing. In 1:22 James contrasts **doers** with **hearers only.** There it is clear, however, that while James says doers, he really means hearers who are also doers, hearers whose hearing produces action; and such hearers whose hearing produces corresponding action in their lives are contrasted with those who are only hearers, whose hearing has no influence on what they do. It is the context of 1:22 that makes this clear. So also the context (particularly 2:18) makes it perfectly clear that when James says in 2:24: **You see that a man is justified by works and not by faith alone,** he really means that a person is justified by the works which faith produces and which grow out of faith and not by a so-called faith which has no influence on what one does or how one lives.

At this point it will be useful to discuss in a bit more detail

how Paul and James use the word *faith*. James is contrasting
two types of faith:

FAITH A	FAITH B
faith without works (2:17)	faith demonstrated by works
faith by itself (2:17)	(2:18)
professed faith (2:14)	active faith (2:22)
useless or barren faith	completed faith (2:22)
(2:20)	living faith (2:26)
dead faith (2:17, 26)	

While James uses the word *faith* for what is described in
Column A, he clearly means that it is an inadequate faith, not
really deserving of the term at all. Paul would agree, with
this difference, however—Paul wouldn't even call what is described in Column A faith. He would not use such an exalted
word for what is dead, barren, a mere profession of the lips.
Paul chooses to limit his use of the word faith to that trust
which is active, complete, living (Column B above). Usually
Paul does not make this explicit. The reader must remember
that for Paul faith is always active and living. But in one
passage, Paul uses language very similar to that of James. In
Galatians 5:6 Paul writes: "For in Christ Jesus neither circumcision nor uncircumcision is of any avail, *but faith working
through love* (cf. also the parallel statements in Gal. 6:15 and
1 Cor. 7:19). The difference between Paul and James here is
not a difference of how one is saved. Both would say it is living,
active faith that saves. James, however, also uses the word faith
to describe those claims in Column A. Paul doesn't do that.
James does it because he knows people who are depending on
such an inadequate faith.

In v 25 another example is chosen from the Old Testament
(see the story of Rahab in Josh. 2:1-24 and 6:21-25) to show
that real faith results in action, it puts itself on the line, it
risks all.

The RSV translation (and most other translations as well) of James' final analogy in v 26 is misleading. As the conclusion of what he has wanted to say in vv 14-25 James uses human life as a comparison. The first half of v 26 is the comparison, a figure of speech and the last half is the conclusion to be drawn from the comparison. As the RSV translates it, James is saying: Just as the body is dead when the spirit leaves it, so also faith is dead without works. The parallels in the construction of the sentence make body analogous to faith and spirit to works. This leaves many readers with the impression that just as the spirit is the essence of the body, so works are the essence of faith. But this is not James' point at all, either here or in vv 14-26. James' point rather is that works are the *evidence* of faith (esp. v 18). The body-spirit analogy does not convey this —the spirit is hardly the evidence of the life of body!

The problem is with the word *spirit*. The Greek word here is *pneuma* which has a number of meanings. The basic meaning of *pneuma* is "air," with related meanings such as "wind" and "breath," which are air in motion. Finally a metaphorical, derived meaning for *pneuma* is "spirit." Whenever the word *pneuma* occurs, the translator must choose whether in the specific context the Greek writer meant air, wind, breath, or spirit.

In this case the context and the sense of v 26 require that *pneuma* be translated not "spirit," but "breath"—and some translators do this (cf. the *New English Bible* and the Roman Catholic *New American Bible*). Using "breath" here results not only in clear meaning for v 26 itself, but also corresponds with James' line of argument throughout the entire section. Verse 26 would then read: "For as the body without breath is dead, so faith apart from works is dead."

How was life and death determined in ancient times? By observing whether breathing occurred. Often a piece of glass or a mirror would be held to the mouth so the condensation of the breath, if any were present, could be seen. James is saying then in v 26: Just as breath is the evidence, demonstration, proof of life in a human being, so works are the evidence, demonstration, proof of a living faith. An expanded translation of v 26 will bring this parallelism out: "For as the body apart from breath (the evidence of life) is dead, so faith apart from works (the evidence of faith) is dead" (cf. v 18 also).

In this section, then, James is not so much disagreeing with Paul, as he is with a misunderstood and misrepresented Paul. James does not disagree that it is faith that saves. He merely disagrees that faith can be separated from a changed life. Faith and the works faith produces are as inseparable as two sides of one coin.

Besides the passages from Jesus (Matt. 7:17-21) and Paul (Gal. 5:6) noted above, there are other sections of the New Testament that emphasize the same truth—see Matthew 25:31-46, the exhortations found in Paul's letters (Rom. 6-7; 12-15; Gal. 5:13—6:10; 1 Thess. 4-5), and much of 1 John.

■ Warnings and Advice to Those Who Teach (3:1-18)

While this section is not closely related to the preceding, it does reflect James' general concern with faith as a vital force that shapes, controls, and changes our lives (cf. 1:19-27; Chapter 2).

The theme of teaching (3:1) ties the two sections of this text together—that on the tongue (3:2-12), the means by which one teaches; and that on true wisdom (3:13-18), the quality of teachers and the content of their instruction. Such associations are common in Old Testament, Rabbinic, and Greek thought, along with frequent warnings as to the serious responsibilities of those who seek to teach others, such as are found here (3:1). The reference is not only to professional teachers, but also to all who on any occasion feel inclined to instruct others.

The Difficulty of Controlling the Tongue (3:1-12)

James first notes the great potential of the tongue (vv 2-5a) and then points out how all too often it is a potential for great evil (vv 5b-8). He concluded by calling attention to the incongruity of our use of our tongues with our new life in Christ (vv 9-12).

In v 2 the writer reminds would-be teachers that all make mistakes and the sign of maturity is the ability to control one's speech.

The analogies, taken from the main forms of transportation in those days, of bridle (v 3) and the rudder (v 4) are positive and emphasize the great potential of the tongue. This potential, however, can be used for good or evil (cf. vv 10-12, also Prov. 18:21: "Death and life are in the power of the tongue"). It is this potential for evil that is uppermost in the writer's mind, as v 5b (which serves as a transition to the next section) already intimates.

What we say both grows out of and influences what we are. James here reflects a kind of thinking that is similar to Jesus' statements about what defiles a person in Mark 7:20ff.

Further, of course, the tongue also has far-reaching effects in the lives of others—indeed, how great a forest can be set ablaze by a match or spark of fire (v 5b).

James (v 6) now spells out in some detail the great potential for evil in the tongue. This is one of the hardest verses to understand and many commentators feel inclined to change the text. The first difficult phrase is **an unrighteous world.** For James "world" is a negative term (cf. 4:4), meaning the world without God, under the control of God's enemy, hostile to God and goodness. In this usage, he reflects a form of dualism found also in John (14:17, 22; 15:18f.; 18:36) and Paul (1 Cor. 1:20; Rom. 12:2). It also parallels very closely Paul's negative understanding of "flesh" as seen in Romans 7 and Galatians 5:16-21. Such an evil power within a person is the tongue, James says.

The second phrase in this verse that is hard to understand is **the cycle of nature.** The RSV gives as an alternative translation "wheel of birth"; another possible translation could be "cycle of becoming." The translation "wheel of birth" suggests the ideas of rebirth and reincarnation (which were found at that time in Egyptian, Greek, and Far-Eastern thought and may be reflected in John 9:2); but more probably this strange phrase is a way of designating "the whole of a person's life and experiences" (cf. Dibelius, *James,* pp. 196-198).

The tongue is not inherently evil but has been **set on fire by hell.** The Greek word for hell is *Gehenna,* a transliteration of a Hebrew phrase, the valley of Hinnom. This valley lies on the south side of Jerusalem and is the garbage dump for the city. With its constant burning and smoking, in the last centuries before the birth of Jesus this valley became a symbol of the apocalyptic place of punishment for the wicked, the final abode of evil and evildoers.

Such a tongue, influenced and dominated by hell itself, is beyond human control (vv 7-8). This is, of course, hyperbole; for all do at times control their tongues. It should not be pressed any more than the hyperbolic claim that every kind of animal had been tamed (v 7). This exaggerated way of speaking serves to impress indelibly on the reader's mind the great and terrible potential for evil of which human speech is capable (v 9).

But change can occur. Therefore James writes of the danger and seeks to motivate the reader to want to alter things. He seeks to do this by showing how incongruous such uncontrolled use of the tongue is in the lives of people made new in Christ (vv 10-12).

No merely human effort can effect this change (v 8); but James has earlier pointed his readers to the source of a power that can make them perfect (mature) if they but choose to use it (1:4-5; cf. also 3:17).

The figures of the grapes and figs (v 12) recall Jesus' words in Matthew 7:16-17. The writer's use of **we** (v 9) includes actual teachers like himself, as well as all those who seek to be such in any situation.

True Wisdom (3:13-18)

James now turns to the quality of teachers and the content of their instruction. Verse 13 directs a challenge to all who would aspire to wisdom and to the position of teaching others— let your lives demonstrate the reality of your wisdom. Verses 14-16 contrast false, earthly wisdom with that wisdom which has its origin in God (vv 17-18).

For James it is not what one *claims*, but what one *does* on the basis of those claims that is all important (v 13). In this he is reiterating his dominant religious stance (cf. 1:22-27; 2:12-13; 2:14-26)—actions speak louder than words.

The characteristics of false wisdom are arrogance, jealousy, ambition (v 14) and contentiousness (v 16). The source of such false wisdom is demonic (v 15). It originates from the world (**earthly**) dominated by God's enemy (**devilish**) and panders to the base animal drives and desires within us (**unspiritual**).

In contrast, true wisdom has its origin **from above** (v 17; cf. also v 15 and 1:5, 17). James here follows the Old Testament wisdom tradition which sees one's relation to God as the source of all wisdom and of all wise living (Prov. 9:10; 2:6-20).

This true wisdom is characterized by the very opposite qualities such as meekness (v 13), gentleness, reasonableness, sincerity, peaceableness, purity, and mercy (v 17)—the very characteristics of the truly religious person noted earlier (1:9, 27; 2:13). The contrasts here recall Paul's similar antitheses between the works of the flesh and the fruits of the Spirit in Galatians 5:19-23.

Verse 18 is connected to the preceding by the references to **peace.** The peace James desires (in contrast to strife and contentiousness) produces a climate of righteousness, i.e., right relationships and right living which are characterized by the qualities mentioned in the previous verse. This verse is transitional to Chapter 4 as well.

■ Miscellaneous Warnings (4:1—5:6)

In these verses James gives a series of warnings to be followed finally with a more positive series of admonitions (5:7-20). First he warns his readers against the dangers of too great an attachment to the world (4:1-10); then against speaking evil of others (4:11-12) and against arrogance (4:13-17). Finally he warns the irreligious rich of the impending judgment (5:1-6).

Against Friendship with the World (4:1-10)

Two concepts in v 1 need comment. **Wars** and **fightings** are meant metaphorically, referring to the long-term, festering strife and the violent outbreaks of open conflict.

The phrase, **in your members,** can be taken literally as referring to the inner conflicts caused by the struggle between the old desires and the new life in Christ. "Members" may also be understood in the Pauline sense of the church as the body of Christ and thus refer to conflicts in the Christian community.

Such self-striving results in conflicts (v 2), the viciousness of which are expressed metaphorically by the word **kill** (though it is also possible that an early scribal error is involved here: Greek *phoneuete* "you kill" may have been misread for a word similar in appearance and sound, *phthoneite* "you are envious").

In reality, however, James reminds that all things could be theirs if they would seek in the proper way—by prayer (v 2b—recall 1:5, 17f.); but such prayer must be in conformity with the new being, not the old, selfish animal desires (v 3). The word for **passions** in Greek does not have negative connotations in itself; but these human, animal desires can become demonic,

all-consuming, and then they become destructive—of self and
of others.

This possibility of our natural desires and self-interest becoming a demonic and all-consuming force in our lives leads
James into a discussion of loyalties and commitment (vv 4-5).
He follows this with an indication of the sources available to his
readers to enable them to remain committed to God (vv 6-10).

In v 4 the term **unfaithful creatures** is actually "adulteresses"
in Greek. This use of the feminine is a metaphor taken from
frequent Old Testament usage (Jer. 3:20; Hos. 9:1) and found
also in Jesus' sayings in the Gospels (Matt. 12:39; 16:4; Mark
8:38). It grows out of the concept of Israel as the wife and bride
of Yahweh (Isa. 54:5f.; Hos. 1-3) and is preserved in the New
Testament image of the church as the bride of Christ (2 Cor.
11:1f.; Eph. 5:24-32; Rev. 19:7; 21:9) and indicates the exclusive
commitment and devotion God demands of his people.

Such exclusive loyalty allows no other center in life; there-
fore, James writes: **friendship with the world is enmity with
God.** Here is a call for radical decision, very similar to what
Jesus says in Matthew 6:24 (cf. vv 19-24; cf. also Luke 16:1-13).
James confronts his readers with a sharp either/or—God or the
world. These are mutually exclusive.

Now James is not saying that the world is automatically evil.
He is not denying that it is God's creation for human care and
use. But James uses **world** here as Jesus uses mammon in Matthew 6:24. World here means the world apart from God, the
world that can become demonic in its influence over us, con-
suming all our time and energy. The choice is between the
world as servant or master. Or, to put it another way, we must
choose who shall be master in our lives—the world or the God
who made it.

Verse 5 is difficult. First of all the words in quotation marks
in the RSV are not found anywhere in Scripture; yet the Greek
construction implies that they are a direct quote. It is possible

that James here is quoting some writing which is unknown to us.

Spirit also is ambiguous. It can either be the subject or object of the sentence in Greek and further it can either mean the Holy Spirit or the human spirit. Thus the following translations are all possible:

a) **He** (God) **yearns jealously over the spirit which he has made to dwell in us.**

b) (Our) spirit which he has made to dwell in us yearns jealously (for him).

c) The (Holy) Spirit which he has made to dwell in us yearns jealously (for our full devotion).

The sense of the entire passage favors either a) or b) and clearly is meant to emphasize the exclusive devotion which properly belongs to God.

In vv 6-10 James points his readers to the source that can enable such total commitment and faithful devotion—the grace of God. This grace God can only give to those who are humble (vv 6, 10), those who admit their helplessness and need of God and who seek his help.

Grace here is the continuing grace God gives to those he has already made his own in Christ. James is addressing Christian people who have already been brought forth **of his own will** by the word of truth to be the first fruits of his creatures (1:18).

The quotation here is from Proverbs 3:34 and is also found in 1 Peter 5:5-9 in a context strikingly similar to James 4:6-10. This indicates that both writers are drawing on a popular Christian tradition concerning the humility and grace needed for the ongoing struggle in the Christian life.

In the following exhortations (vv 8-10), it must be remembered that James is addressing those to whom God has already drawn near and in whom he has already begun his new work (1:18, 2-4; 2:1). As they struggle to remain faithful to God, James challenges, warns, exhorts, admonishes as is common in all Christian instruction (cf. e.g., Gal. 5:13-26; Rom. 6:12-19;

12:1ff.; Heb. 12:1–13:6); for part of God's new creation in us is a new will that needs to be addressed and challenged. This exercise of moral effort on the part of those whom he has won to himself, is part of God's grace—the way he has chosen to enable us to change and grow. Paul has expressed well the tension implied here by James. Paul addresses the Christians at Philippi: "Work out your own salvation with fear and trembling; for God is at work in you, both to will and to accomplish his good pleasure" (Phil. 2:12b-13).

Against Speaking Evil of Others (4:11-12)

Closely related to the conflicts mentioned in 4:1-2 is the slander and the judging of one another that James condemns in this section. In this he is following an important New Testament motif (cf. Matt. 7:1-5; Rom. 2:1-3; 14:3-13). James' line of argumentation in the last half of v 11 recalls his method of reasoning in 2:8-13, and implies that judgmental people have set themselves above and outside the law (cf. Paul similarly in Rom. 2:1-3). It is God's prerogative, and God's alone, to judge (Rom. 12:4).

To the Arrogant (4:13-17)

James follows up now with another evidence of arrogance— the feeling that we control our own destiny; the inability or unwillingness to admit our dependence on God every day of our lives (v 13).

We are creatures, limited and at the mercy of the ambiguities and uncertainties of life (v 14). This need not lead us to despair, but should rather turn us daily in our dependence to God (v 15) rather than to an arrogant and false self-sufficiency (v 16).

James then gives a solemn warning, suggesting that those arrogant people are not acting innocently or out of ignorance, but in full awareness; they are deliberately rejecting God from their lives (v 17).

To the Rich (5:1-6)

James continues here a theme dealt with elsewhere in his letter—condemnation of the impious rich and advocacy for the misused righteous poor. Earlier, he had warned the wealthy that life and riches are transient (1:9-11; 4:13f.) and noted that often they oppress the righteous poor (2:6-7).

In this section, he emphasizes the misery that awaits them, including the loss of their possessions upon which they falsely base their security (5:1-3a) and warns them that their often ill-gotten gains and luxurious ways will accuse them in the final judgment (5:3b-6).

How is this reference to the **rich** in v 1 to be understood? It is possible that they are not members of the Christian community and are condemned in absentia. It seems more probable, however, that the author of James here reflects an awareness of a growing toleration and courting of the rich throughout the church (cf. 2:1-7), even by congregational leaders. Thus James uses this occasion to castigate the rich and, by implication, the leaders and attitudes that curry their favor.

Miseries that are coming upon you is best taken (in the light of vv 3, 5, and 8-9 in the next section) as a reference to the final judgment conceived of as imminent (cf. esp. vv 8-9).

The tenses in the RSV translation of vv 2-3 fluctuate between the present, perfect, and the future. All three tenses are to be understood as future, with both the perfect and the present tenses being used to portray the certainty of their final yet imminent condemnation.

The reference to **gold and silver** rusting (v 3) is no doubt deliberate, to emphasize that even their most prized possessions which seem so permanent are as insubstantial as all other material things. In this section James echoes Jesus' statement in Matthew 6:19-20.

The last half of v 3 is transitional to the next segment (which catalogs the accusers of the rich on the last day) and makes the striking point here that the very things (silver and gold) on which they rely for security will become evidence against them!

The RSV translation *for the last days* represents the most probable understanding of the Greek preposition *en;* however, it would also be possible to translate the *en* as "*in* the last days." This would imply that right now, even as this letter is being composed, the rich continue their inordinate heaping up of illicit gains and their misguided pursuit of security.

How striking is the ironic use of laying up **treasure** here! They think they are amassing lasting wealth and security, but in reality they are treasuring up condemnation and punishment for themselves (cf. Jesus' vivid descriptions in Luke 16:19-31 and Matt. 25:31-46).

Two condemnations are laid at the doorstep of the rich in vv 4-5. First of all, their unjust exploitation of the defenseless poor (v 4) cries out to heaven for vindication like Abel's blood of old (cf. Gen. 4:10). This withholding of wages is frequently castigated in the Old Testament (cf. Lev. 19:13; Deut. 24:14f.; Mal. 3:5). Second, their life of luxury and pleasure (v 5), which James criticized earlier (1:27; 2:14-16) reflects lack of concern for human need, and makes the rich like sleek, fatted cattle ready for slaughter. This vivid metaphor echoes the descriptions of Amos (esp. 4:1-3 and frequently throughout the entire book).

In this, and other sections of his writing, James shows an awareness of the situation of the church in the last half of the first Christian century when there were more and more wealthy converts to the faith. James here reflects the more caustic and radical criticism of the wealthy found in Luke's beatitudes (Luke 6:20-26), which are toned down and domesticized in the later and more familiar Matthean version (Matt. 5:3-6).

While this condemnation of the rich seems absolute, with no hope for change, it may actually be a portrayal of their fate which is meant to shock them out of their complacency so they will repent and turn to God before it is too late. In any case this is also a warning to the entire congregation of the danger of riches so that they will neither envy wealth nor vainly pursue it.

Such radical statements, as we see here in James and elsewhere in Scripture, do not indicate that the Bible condemns wealth in itself; rather such statements are meant to point up most impressively the perils that accompany the abundance of material blessings and the grave responsibilities that attend their possession.

■ Miscellaneous Admonitions (5:7-20)

In this final section of his letter the author now speaks in a more positive tone of encouragement and admonition. He seeks to strengthen the faithful in their common life in the congregation as they wait for the return of the Lord Jesus (5:7-12). Then he reminds them of the tremendous power of prayer (5:13-18) and encourages them to greater care and concern for the erring in their midst (5:19-20).

Concerning Patience Until the Lord Returns (5:7-12)

The motif of the end of the world is now viewed from its more positive side, namely, of deliverance for God's faithful. This motif is used to encourage God's people patiently to endure the injustice and wrongs noted in the previous section, knowing their vindication is as certain as the rains needed for the maturing of the crops.

The **coming of the Lord** (vv 7-8) translates the Greek word *parousia* (which has come over into English intact). This is a technical term referring to Christ's return at the end of the world. James says this return of Christ is **at hand.** He here reflects the common belief among Christians of the first century that Jesus would return during their lifetime (cf. also

1 Thess. 4:14f.; Rom. 16:20; 1 Cor. 7:29-31), echoing the words of Jesus himself (Mark 13:29).

While the church was mistaken in this expectation that Christ would return in their generation, the admonitions to steadfast confidence in God for his faithfulness are still very relevant.

In v 10 James refers to a Jewish/Christian tradition of prophet-martyrs (cf. for example Ezek. 14:14, 20; Matt. 23:29-31; Heb. 11:32-38). He follows this with a reference to the **steadfastness of Job,** the action of a courageous spirit that, despite inexplicable suffering and unanswered doubts, holds fast to the certainty of faith and confidence in God (cf. Job 13:15).

The word **purpose** (v 11) translates the Greek word *telos* which literally means "end." This has led some commentators to find in this phrase a reference to a third example of steadfastness, namely Jesus Christ. But this is improbable since there is no preparation in the text for this shift. The word *telos* can be translated "purpose" as the RSV does, but it is more likely that the writer intends the meaning "end" and has in mind Job 42:12: "and the Lord blessed the latter *end* (Hebrew text) of Job more than his beginning."

Verse 12 is an isolated saying with little connection with what precedes or follows. It is a piece of tradition very similar to Jesus' words concerning the taking of oaths in Matthew 5:33-37 (but James may reflect an earlier form of the tradition than Matthew—cf. Dibelius, *James,* 250f.). Oaths were very common and often taken lightly; therefore this abuse is not infrequently castigated by Jews and Greeks alike. Thus the admonition by James (and Jesus) that a simple yes or no should be sufficient. Because this is a traditional bit of advice, perhaps the **above all** need not be pressed.

Concerning Prayer (5:13-18)

Earlier James had discussed the right kind of prayer (1:5-8 and 4:2b-3); here he tells his readers that prayer is for all situations in their lives (v 13); for all of life is to be related to God (cf. also Eph. 5:18b-20; Phil. 4:11-13).

In vv 14-16a, James deals with the relationship of prayer to sickness and healing. In v 14, the anointing of the sick with oil seems to be a Jewish practice, mentioned only here and in Mark 6:13 in the entire New Testament. It is unclear whether the oil itself was thought to have therapeutic value or whether James is reflecting Jewish practices concerning exorcisms, since sickness was generally considered to be caused by demons and/or sin. In any case, the church for many centuries followed the practice of anointing with oil to restore the sick to health. It was only much later (about the ninth century) that such anointing became a ritual of preparation for death (the practice of Extreme Unction in the Roman Catholic Church).

In vv 15 and 16, two aspects warrant comment. First of all sin and sickness seem to be intimately related. It should be noted that in v 15b it is stated **if he has committed sins . . . .** This suggests that James did not hold the general rabbinical view that all sickness was the result of a person's sins ("No one gets up from his bed of sickness until all his sins have been forgiven"—Rabbi Alexander). That Jesus and/or the disciples held the view that in some cases sin and sickness may be related, seems to be indicated in passages like John 9:1-3 and Mark 2:3-5. We today no longer make this association; yet a truth is reflected in this ancient view—there cannot be complete health of body and mind until a person is in a right relationship with God.

Finally v 15 seems to suggest that prayer for healing will always result in restored health. The verb **will save** should not be taken in an absolute sense, as though giving the one who prays irresistible control over God (even Paul did not have this kind of power—cf. his fervent but unfulfilled request for healing in 2 Cor. 12:7-10). **Will save** is best understood here, as a forceful way of saying that it is prayer and the power God chooses to make available in response to prayer that accomplishes this healing. Healing does not depend on the medicinal value of the oil or on the ritual of anointing.

The concern for physical healing reflected in this passage has always been a dominant concern of the church—evidenced throughout the writings of the early church fathers and seen in our day in the establishment of hospitals and clinics wherever the church has gone throughout the world.

In vv 16b-18, James shows by the example of Elijah, **a man of like nature with ourselves** (v 17), just how effective and powerful prayer can be. The story of Elijah in the Old Testament (1 Kings 17 and 18) does not actually say that Elijah prayed in this instance. Rabbinic exegesis, however, found evidence of prayer in the statements that Elijah was "standing" before God (1 Kings 17:1) and later "threw himself down upon the earth and put his face between his knees" (1 Kings 18:42). James is probably following a Jewish exegetical tradition here, as he seems also to have done in speaking of **three years and six months** (v 17) instead of the three years of the biblical text (1 Kings 18:1). Luke 4:25 also speaks of three years and six months, apparently reflecting the same Jewish tradition.

Concern for the Erring (5:19-20)

These final verses deal with one of the most serious problems in the early church—the problem of apostasy. In a time of persecution (1:2-4, 12), as well as in periods of moral laxity (1:13-15), the temptation to turn away from the faith is always strong. That this was such a time is clear from other New Testament writings stemming from the same period (cf., for example, Heb. 2:1-4; 13:7-13 and especially 6:1-8; cf. also Matt. 24:9-10; 2 Tim. 4:10; 2 Peter 3:17).

The writer concludes his letter by appealing to his readers not to give up on those who have left their fellowship, but rather to seek to win them back once more (v 19), pointing out the immeasurable benefits of such saving activity (v 20).

The person referred to by **his** in the phrase, **will save his soul**

from death, has often been debated. While there are Rabbinic parallels that indicate his might refer to the person who wins the apostate back (and thereby saves his own soul), it is more probable that James here refers to the soul of the apostate who has been delivered thereby from death (in the sense of eternal condemnation—cf. 1:15; 4:4, 12; 5:1-6).

A similar ambiguity is found in the final phrase, **will cover a multitude of sins.** Whose sins are meant? Those of the apostate or of those who win the apostate back? Actually there are three ways to take this phrase. If the writer is quoting or alluding to Proverbs 10:12 "love covers all offenses," the meaning would be: love will excuse the sinners and put the best construction on all that they do, rather than passing harsh judgments upon them (cf. James 2:13). This appears to be the meaning of the same passage in 1 Peter 4:8.

Or the reference may be that the love and concern that wins the apostate back will have this good result—that it effects forgiveness and life for the sinner. This may be the meaning here, emphasizing the mutual care and concern of the Christian community.

If, however, James reflects Jewish traditions, he may mean that one who wins another person back covers up one's own sins. In Tobit 4:10 and elsewhere the idea is expressed that good deeds and evil deeds are balanced off against one another in the heavenly accounts.

It is possible to interpret the 1 Peter 4:8 passage in this way also. While the Christian reader will note (and lament) the lack of any explicit reference to the atoning work of Jesus in connection with forgiveness in this passage, it is well to remember that James does point to God's forgiveness and grace as it is mediated in and through the Christian community (cf., for example, 2:13 and the references to baptism in 1:18 and 2:7). This note of grace is surely a fitting conclusion to a writing which reflects so deep a concern for the new life which has been made possible in Jesus Christ.

ABOUT THE AUTHOR

R. A. Martin is a graduate of Wartburg Seminary, Dubuque, Iowa. His Th.D. in biblical studies is from Princeton. Prof. Martin served as a missionary and professor in India 1957-1969. Since 1969 he has been professor of biblical studies at Wartburg Seminary.

I PETER

John H. Elliott

INTRODUCTION

For Christians throughout the ages the letter of 1 Peter has represented one of the highlights of New Testament proclamation. In his first translation of the original biblical texts into the common language of the German people, Martin Luther ranked 1 Peter among "the true and noblest books of the New Testament." Together with John's Gospel, and Paul's letters to the Romans, the Galatians, and the Ephesians, Luther listed 1 Peter among

> the books that show you Christ and teach you all that is necessary and salvatory for you to know, even if you were never to see or hear any other book or doctrine. . . . For in them you do not find many works and miracles of Christ described, but you do find depicted in masterly fashion how faith in Christ overcomes sin, death, and hell, and gives life, righteousness, and salvation. (*Luther's Works*, Vol. 35, pp. 361-62.)

This high estimate of 1 Peter as a demonstration of the real nature of the gospel seems consistent with the church's attitude from the early period onward. Since the end of the first century Christian authors such as Clement of Rome (1 Clement) and Bishop Polycarp of Smyrna in Asia Minor (Polycarp to the Philippians) were inspired by its words of consolation, exhortation, and hope. In the following centuries it was quickly and universally embraced in both the West and the East as an indisputable statement of the church's faith, teaching, and practice.

Since the advent of modern biblical study, 1 Peter has met with a more mixed reaction. For some commentators this letter contains "a gallant and high-hearted exhortation which breathes a spirit of undaunted courage and exhibits as noble a type of piety as can be found in any writing of the New Testament outside the gospels, . . . a microcosm of Christian faith and duty, the model of a pastoral charge." For others it reflects a late New Testament document modeled after but inferior to the correspondence of Paul. In regard to the many historical, literary, and theological questions which this letter poses, it is no understatement to say that 1 Peter currently represents a "storm-centre of New Testament studies" (Stephen Neill, *The Interpretation of the New Testament 1861-1961*, London: Oxford, 1964, p. 343).

Given the vigorous debate concerning virtually every aspect of 1 Peter's composition—its literary form, author and addressees, place and date of origin, historical situation, affinities with other New Testament writings, the nature and strategy of its theological and social message—the positions outlined in this commentary can only be regarded as provisional. Our aim is to analyze the questions this document poses and the information suggested in the text that might lead to some answers. Our aim, however, is not merely to solve textual problems but to discover how these early Christian writings communicated the good news of salvation to the people of their own generation.

1. Literary Form, Integrity and Use of Tradition

1 Peter manifests all the essential features of a conventional Greek letter. It opens with a salutation (1:1-2), continues with the message proper (1:3–5:11) and concludes with a commendation of its probable bearer, Silvanus, and the personal greetings of the senders (5:12-14). This letter makes rich use of a

broad stream of early Christian tradition. This is evident in the similarities between 1 Peter and many other New Testament writings. There are points of contact with

• the Gospels (significance of Jesus' death and resurrection; words of the Lord regarding trust in God as Father; humility and service within the community, and joy in suffering)

• Acts (speeches and narratives involving Peter, Silvanus-Silas, and Mark)

• the epistles of Paul (esp. Rom., 1 Thess., Eph., 1 Tim., and Titus concerning the household image of the church, Christian suffering and moral behavior)

• Hebrews (Christian alienation in society)

• James (common use of Old Testament texts, joy in suffering, trust in God)

• 1 John (Christian brotherhood and familial exhortation) and

• Revelation (suffering of Christ and Christians and common use of Old Testament texts).

Such similarities indicate not that 1 Peter copied from other literature, but that all these writings drew upon an extensive Christian oral tradition. To this tradition belonged

1) clusters of Old Testament texts appropriate for describing Jesus as the suffering Servant-Messiah and his believers as the people of God;

2) authoritative words of the Lord;

3) catechetical instruction on the meaning and moral requirements of baptism;

4) creeds or hymns proclaiming the advent-suffering-death-resurrection-exaltation of Jesus Christ as Lord;

5) symbols of community;

6) patterns of moral exhortation; and

7) liturgical practices which Christians received and developed from their Jewish heritage.

The amount of such tradition in 1 Peter is so great in fact
that some scholars regard the original form of this document
as a baptismal sermon (1:3–4:11) to which 1:1-2 and 4:12–
5:14 were added later. Others propose that 1 Peter incorporates
an early Christian liturgy, or even that it represents the cele-
brant's portion of an Easter baptismal eucharist. Explicit mention is indeed made of baptism in 3:21 and baptismal allusions
and instruction abound in 1 Peter. Similarly, the Greek word
for "suffering" *(paschein)* bears a similarity to the Greek term
for "passover" *(pascha)*.

On the whole, however, such theories have proved too specu-
lative to be convincing. For one thing, no further contemporary
examples of such proposed homilies or liturgies are available.
Furthermore, reference is made to baptism in order to remind
and reassure the believers of the implications of their conversion. They are not in the act of being baptized but have already
been reborn (1:3), and have become believers in Jesus Christ
(2:4-10) and children of God (1:14). Their baptism continues
to be the sign of their salvation *now* (3:21) in the present hour
of their affliction (3:13-17). Such references to affliction and
suffering are not part of a liturgical commemoration of Jesus'
suffering on Golgotha but are acknowledgments of the actual
suffering of the believers which unify them with both the
suffering and the glory of their risen Lord (3:18-22; 4:12-19).

Further traces of liturgical tradition such as the Christological creedal or hymnic formulas in 1:20, 2:21-25, and 3:18-22,
or the doxologies and "amens" in 4:11 and 5:11 or the kiss of
peace in 5:14, similarly reveal more about the nature and content of Christian worship at the time of 1 Peter's composition
than about the form of 1 Peter's composition in particular.
1 Peter is best regarded as a genuine letter in which abundant
use has been made of Christian tradition to express the bonds
that unite senders and recipients and provide the basis for
encouragement and exhortation.

2. Destination

The salutation of 1 Peter indicates that it was addressed to "visiting strangers" (RSV: **exiles**) **of the Dispersion in Pontus, Galatia, Cappadocia, Asia, and Bithynia** (1:1). These five names refer to originally independent territories of Asia Minor (present-day Turkey) which since ca. 130 B.C. through bequest or annexation had fallen to Roman control in its gradual conquest of the entire Mediterranean world. The topography of Asia Minor, its rivers, lakes, and mountain ranges extending east-west across the northern and southern sections of this land mass, created natural boundaries which preserved the rich political and cultural diversity of its population. By the time of 1 Peter these names referred to the provinces Rome had created. Bithynia and Pontus were united as one province since 62 B.C.

However, except for the coastal areas and the province of Asia, Greek and Roman influence here remained minimal, especially in the vast isolated rural interior. Totaling an area of about 129,000 square miles, these four provinces comprised all of Asia Minor north and west of the Taurus Mountains. Its overall population of ca. 8.5 million comprised an estimated one million Jews and 80,000 Christians by the end of the first Christian century. Outside of Syria-Palestine it was in Asia Minor that the Christian movement made its earliest and most extensive advance.

Galatia and Asia were fields of the Pauline mission in the first half of the 50s. But for Bithynia-Pontus and Cappadocia there is no evidence of Pauline activity or influence. The predominantly rural character of the areas addressed in 1 Peter and the rural imagery employed in the letter (e.g., metaphors from agriculture, herding, military outposts [1:4; 5:3] and comparison of the enemy with a ravenous lion, 5:8) likewise contrast to the urban centers of Pauline activity and the corresponding urban imagery for the church which Paul employed.

Moreover, there were missionaries at work in Asia Minor apart
from Paul and his associates. Therefore, there is little basis for
assuming that 1 Peter was addressed to Pauline congregations
and, for this reason, that the letter should be regarded as a
development of the peculiar Pauline kerygma. As its content
and message also reveal, 1 Peter points to Christian activity
simultaneous with Paul yet independent of his work and
writing.

The *persons* addressed in 1 Peter, as in all the New Testament writings, were converts from both Jewish and Gentile
segments of society. Indicative of the former is the use of the
Jewish Scriptures (1:16, 24; 2:3, 4-10, 22-25; 3:10-12, 14; 4:18;
5:5), reference to venerated Hebrew persons (Abraham and
Sarah, 3:6; the prophets, 1:10-12), important events in Hebrew-
Jewish history (Passover, 1:13 and the Exodus, 1:18-19; exile,
Babylon in 5:13) and terms of honor applied to the ancient
people of God (**holy,** 1:14-16; 3:5, "elect," 1:1; 5:13 and esp.
2:4-10). For former Jews or former converts to Judaism, such
tradition would have the most meaning and weight. On the
other hand, mention of former Gentile ignorance of God's will,
isolation from God, and traits typical of pagan behavior and
association (1:14, 18; 2:10; 4:2-4) also indicate the presence
of a significant number of non-Jews among the intended
recipients.

Among the recipients are **free men** (2:16), household slaves
(2:18-20), wives with non-believing husbands (3:1-6) and husbands with Christian wives (3:7), community leaders-elders
(5:1-4) and recent converts ("younger persons," 5:5). Perhaps
the most significant clue to the social (including legal and economic) status of the addressees is their designation as "visiting
strangers" (1:1; 2:11) and "resident aliens" (2:11, cf. 1:17). In
ancient society strangers were regarded with a mixture of fear
and contempt. With their peculiar accents, their weird cus-
toms and alien (religious) rites, strangers were constantly
viewed as threats to established order and native well-being.

Greek and Roman epics such as the *Odyssey* and the *Aeneid* as well as the Old Testament history of God's company of aliens reflect the perilous plight of the stranger in a strange land. Strangers were "outsiders," relegated to the margin of society by native law and social forms of discrimination.

The Greek term behind the RSV **exiles** in 1 Peter 2:11 is a technical term meaning "resident aliens" *(paroikoi)*. In the Greco-Roman world of the day this term designated a class of people considered inferior to the full citizens and accorded only limited legal and social rights. Such resident aliens, as in modern national regulations, were prohibited from voting and also from owning land (the major source of income); they were restricted in marriage, inheritance of property, and in commercial transactions with full citizens.

In Asia Minor some of these social outsiders lived in the cities where they carried on their trades. The majority, however, resided in the rural regions of the interior where as peasants gathered in the household communities of the villages they worked the land. Because of the social discrimination they experienced, similar to that experienced by the successive waves of immigrants to the shores of the United States, they frequently formed clubs and labor guilds for the sake of protection, support, and acceptance. Such associations often involved religious worship as well.

The resident aliens addressed in 1 Peter had turned to Christianity as a form of human community that provided not only the social unity and acceptance they lacked but also the favor and acceptance of the God of Israel who "sets the solitary in families." Having embraced the Christian faith through baptism, however, they soon began to realize that membership in this sect provided no escape from the prejudices and pressures of an alien society. To the contrary, adherence to this strange and exclusive movement from the East only meant an increase in social conflict with their neighbors.

3. The Social and Theological Situation and the Strategy of 1 Peter

This letter is an exceptional example of how the "good news of salvation" was set forth with regard to the social and religious conditions of the early Christians. It is designed as a word of consolation and encouragement for Christians suffering as a result of social discrimination and alienation; its aim is to motivate its readers to resist pressures for social conformity and to stand fast in faith, hope, and love.

Motivated by curiosity (3:15), **ignorance** (2:15), and suspicion of wrongdoing (2:12; 4:14-16) and civic disloyalty (2:13-17) on the part of those whom they had labeled "Christians" (lit. Christ-lackeys), the non-Christians had begun to slander, reproach and abuse the believers (2:12; 3:13; 4:14). The termination of social bonds and cultic ties had produced not only a sense of estrangement but also an angry denunciation of the Christians and their God (4:4). Such hostility had engendered sorrow (1:6; 2:19), **fear** (3:14) and **suffering** (2:19, 20; 3:14, 17; 4:1, 14-15, 19; 5:9, 10) among the believers. Under such pressures the Christians were in danger of doubting the benefits of conversion, of renouncing their faith in God's mercies, and of forsaking their communal ties with their fellow believers.

In the face of pressures to conform to the culture around them—a move which would have meant the very demise of this sect in Asia Minor—the addressees are reminded that baptism and faith made them a unique community and that their conversion required them to separate from the non-believers.

In response to the waning of hope caused by suffering, 1 Peter reassures the recipients of God's faithfulness, his judgment of the righteous and the unrighteous, and his vindication of those who remain faithful. The letter reminds its audience of their common election and divine call, of their participation in the suffering of their resurrected Lord, and of their life of holy obedience to God made possible through the sanctifying action of the Holy Spirit.

The letter takes seriously the strangeness of the Christian community and, in addition, provides a theological reason for remaining aliens *(paroikoi)*. God, the Wholly Other One, has made these strangers **holy** (1:14-16) through the holy **blood of Christ** (1:18-19) and has gathered them into a spiritual family which is wholly different in its origin and goal from the natural or political families of mankind. Like Israel of old, the letter affirms, they too are strangers in society, and strangers they are to remain, so that the distinctive nature of the Christian gospel might achieve its ultimate goal, namely, the glorification of this holy God by all humanity (2:12).

Although the term "church" *(ekklesia)* itself is never used, in the broader theological sense 1 Peter is one of the most church-oriented compositions in the New Testament. Various traditional images depict the identity and responsibilities of the Christian community such as

- **flock of God** and "shepherding" (2:25; 5:1-4),

- "fellowship" with Christ in suffering (4:1, 12-13; 5:1),

- incorporation **in Christ** (3:16; 5:10, 14), and

- the epithets for God's elect and holy people combined in 2:9-10.

However, the identification and exhortation of the Christians as the *household* or *family of God* dominates the letter from beginning to end. Believers are the "reborn" (1:3, 23; 2:2) **children** (1:14; cf. 2:10) of a heavenly **Father** (1:2, 3, 17; cf. 4:17) united in one **household of God** (2:5; 4:17) or **brotherhood** (2:17; 5:9; see also the familial terms of 5:12-13 and the household pattern of instruction in 2:18–5:5).

This inclusive accent on the familial nature of the Christian community establishes both the connection between its character and calling and the contrast to its condition in society. The social condition and divine vocation of Christians are the two polar focal points of 1 Peter. The good news of this letter in brief is this: although they are strangers and aliens in society,

Christians can be sure of their salvation because of their incorporation in the household of God. The church, according to 1 Peter, is a home for the homeless.

4. Date, Authorship, and Place of Composition

The numerous correspondences between 1 Peter and Romans (c. A.D. 57) and 1 Clement (c. A.D. 96) establish the Roman origin of all three documents as well as the lower and upper limits, respectively, of 1 Peter's date of composition. Both Romans and 1 Clement are indisputably associated with the Christian community at Rome. The similarities between Romans and 1 Peter indicate that while 1 Peter did not directly quote from Romans, this letter was part of the tradition adapted in 1 Peter. The many affinities between 1 Peter and 1 Clement are best explained by similar circumstances: the author of 1 Clement was influenced by the terminology, motifs and perspective of 1 Peter. This means that 1 Peter was written sometime after A.D. 57 and before 96.

Other factors corroborate this general date and help to narrow its limits. The wide scope of the address in 1:1 requires that a sufficient amount of time be allowed for Christianity to spread to this area after the mssion of Paul (c. 50-60). The problem addressed in 1 Peter, moreover, was no longer an internal Jewish debate concerning the Mosaic law as in Paul, but the struggle of a group of believers now labeled "Christians" over against an alien society.

Furthermore, the tradition used in 1 Peter shows a growth and development since the Pauline period. The shift from a positive (Rom. 13) to a neutral stance toward Roman government (1 Peter 2:13-17) would be accounted for by the anti-Christian pogrom undertaken by Nero in Rome (c. 65-67) as viewed from the distance of a decade or more. By the time of 1 Peter the problem at Rome (Christians accused of having set fire to the city) was over. But the anti-Christian actions of

Nero had taught a sobering lesson about overestimating Roman officials as "ministers of God" (Rom. 13:6).

On the other hand, the neutrality of 1 Peter toward Roman government stands in stark contrast to the thoroughly negative assessment of Rome as the agent of Satan in the Revelation to John (written to Christians in one of the same provinces addressed by 1 Peter in A.D. 96). By this last decade of the first century there is, beside Revelation, evidence of anti-Christian initiatives in Rome (by the emperor Domitian, 93-96) and Christian defections in Pontus (the Roman governor Pliny's correspondence with the emperor Trajan, c. A.D. 111/112, referring to Christian apostasy c. A.D. 92). 1 Peter reflects none of these later developments but rather appears to have been written during the relative tranquility of the Flavian imperial period (A.D. 69-92).

A further factor pointing to the post-70 date of 1 Peter and its composition at Rome is the figurative use of the term **Babylon** in 5:13. Since there is no trace of any Petrine activity associated with the ancient city of Babylon in Mesopotamia or the Roman military outpost in Egypt also known as Babylon, it is virtually certain that Babylon in 5:13 refers figuratively to Rome. Here, according to the unanimous testimony of the early church, was the location of Peter's final ministry and martyrdom (c. 65-67). The use of this term as a reference to Rome (with varying implications) occurs only in literature composed after the destruction of Jerusalem, i.e., A.D. 70 (Sibylline Oracles 5:143, 159; 2 Baruch 11:1; 67:7; 4 Ezra 3:1, 38, 31; Rev. 14:8; 16:19, etc.).

All these factors taken together make it likely that 1 Peter was written from Rome sometime in the middle years of the Flavian imperial period, i.e., between c. 75 and 92. Such a dating would be consistent with the relatively simple level of church organization and leadership it implies (4:10-11; 5:1-5), its servant Christology, its Christ-centered motivation for moral conduct, the absence of disputes over heresy, and its lively expectation that the world would soon be coming to an end, all of which relate 1 Peter to other New Testament documents of this same period.

Should such a date of composition seem most likely, it is then clear that Peter himself did not write the letter since according to the most reliable evidence, Peter died a martyr's death in Rome c. A.D. 65-67. The polished literary style of composition and the use of several Greek terms that occur nowhere else in the New Testament are also difficult to reconcile with an unschooled (Acts 4:13) fisherman who was recognizable by his rustic Galilean brogue (see Matt. 26:72). At 5:12, **By Silvanus . . . I have written briefly to you . . .** , could imply that it was actually Silvanus who, as a secretary, wrote the letter under Peter's direction. However, the original Greek expression used here more often identifies an emissary through whom a letter is delivered and is virtually identical to Acts 15:23 where Silas/Silvanus, along with Judas Barsabbas, similarly served as an emissary through whom the letter of the Jerusalem council was sent to the believers at Antioch. It is therefore more likely that the Silvanus, Mark, and unnamed female mentioned in 1 Peter 5:12 and 13 constituted important members of a Petrine group at Rome which was responsible for both the composition and delivery of the letter (on Silvanus and Mark see the commentary on 5:12-14).

1 Peter, then, is Petrine in the sense that it records and transmits the theological heritage and social vision of the apostle who was still recognized after his martyrdom as the leading figure and apostolic authority of the Roman community in which this letter originated. By the period from 75-92, the Christians at Rome would have had time to consolidate locally following the Neronian pogrom. They would also have had opportunity to develop the Petrine vision of a worldwide brotherhood which 1 Peter expresses. In this letter the concern of the Christians at Rome for the unity and solidarity of the Christian movement receives its first articulation.

AN OUTLINE OF 1 PETER

Evidence for the structure of 1 Peter has already been cited in connection with the discussion of its literary form. The letter is a homogenous mixture of description and direction. Thus *who* the Christians are everywhere determines *how* they are to be. Underlying this combined message of encouragement and exhortation is the basic tension between the social condition of the Christians and their divine vocation, their contrast to non-believers and their communion in Christ. In order to elucidate the manner in which this tension between homelessness in society and "at-homeness" with God is addressed in the various sections of the letter, the following paraphrase-outline is offered.

■ *1:1-2 Salutation: The apostle Peter to the elect homeless believers of the Dispersion in Asia Minor: Greeting!*

■ *1:3—2:10 By the mercy of God you strangers in society have become the elect and holy people of God, the household of faith.*

1:3-12 Praise be to God for the saving benefits of his mercy!

- 3-5   *Through the resurrection of Jesus Christ, God the Father has given us new birth to a living hope, an imperishable inheritance, and a sure salvation in this final age.*

- 6-9   *You can rejoice in this fact and await the revelation of this salvation with faith tested by suffering and with love.*

- 10-12   *The good news of salvation which the prophets sought has been revealed now exclusively to you.*

1:13-21   *You, God's holy children, are to lead a distinctive, holy way of life indicative of your hope in God's grace.*

1:22-25   *As a fraternal community purified through obedience to the truth, maintain your unity through constant familial love; for you have been reborn through the enduring word of the good news.*

2:1-3   *Therefore avoid all acts of dissension and continue to feed on the milk of the word, namely, the Lord.*

2:4-10   *It is the Lord Jesus Christ whom you approach in faith, the Elect and Holy One of God, through whom, by God's mercy, you have become the elect and holy community of God, the household of the Spirit.*

■ 2:11–4:11   *As resident aliens and strangers in society, through obedience to God preserve the distinctiveness and solidarity of your household to the glory of God.*

2:11-12   *As the elect and holy household of faith, live as holy strangers in society so that through your* distinctive style of behavior even hostile outsiders (Gentiles) might come to glorify God.

2:13—3:12   Be subordinate because of the Lord to every institution created for humankind.

- 13-17   Be subordinate to civil authority, but love the brotherhood and fear only God.
- 18-20   Household slaves, be subordinate to your owners by doing good, even if you suffer unjustly.
- 21-25   You (household slaves) have been called to follow the Christ who, by also suffering unjustly in subordination to the will of God, has made it possible for you to do the same.
- 3:1-6   Wives, be subordinate to your husbands by doing good and not fearing them.
- 7   Husbands, live in household harmony with your wives and respect them as co-heirs of the grace of life.
- 8-12   All members of the household, maintain the unity of the community; you have been called to avoid evil and do good.

3:13—4:6   Distinguish yourselves by doing good, even in the face of outsiders' hostility; God vindicates the righteous.

- 13-17   If you should be caused to suffer by your detractors, let it be only for the doing of good in obedience to God's will.
- 18-22   Christ the righteous One also suffered innocently. His suffering, death, and resurrection-exaltation is the basis of your salvation and vindication.
- 4:1-6   Separate yourselves from the sinful outsiders who

condemn you. God will condemn them and vindicate
the faithful.

4:7-11   Maintain the solidarity of the household of God
         to the glory of God.

■ 4:12-19 Rejoice in the test which your suffering
           brings for being God's distinctive house-
           hold.

■ 5:1-11   Maintain the unity of the household of
           God, resist the forces of evil, and com-
           mit yourselves to the care of God.

5:1-4   Leaders, be responsible and not selfish shep-
         herds of God's flock.
5:5a   Recent converts, be subordinate to your lead-
         ers.
5:5b-11 All of you, be humble with one another before
         God. Be firm in your resistance to evil. The
         power of God that exalts you will also confirm
         you.

5:12-14 Conclusion and fraternal greetings.

COMMENTARY

1:1-2 Salutation: The apostle Peter to the elect homeless believers of the Dispersion in Asia Minor: Greeting!

The salutation identifies the apostolic figure in whose name and authority this letter from Rome was written, the social condition and locale of its addressees, and three aspects of their elected status before God.

1a—Peter, according to the combined testimony of the New Testament, was one of the leading forces in the life and mission of the early church. Listed first among the disciples called and then sent by Jesus as apostles (Mark 1:16-18; 3:13-19 par.), remembered as first witness of the resurrected Christ (1 Cor. 15:5) and first leader of the Jerusalem church (Acts 1-5), this Galilean fisherman, Simon son of John (Matt. 16:17; John 1:42), eventually became known as Simon Peter or simply Peter. ("Peter is derived from the Greek *Petros* which translated the Aramaic nickname *Kepha* ["Rock"] which Jesus had given him.) First also, along with Philip, to extend the good news to the Gentiles in coastal Palestine (Acts 10-11), he subsequently traveled to Antioch (Gal. 2:11-14), possibly Corinth (1 Cor. 1:12; 3:22; 9:5) and finally to Rome where, according to early tradition (e.g., 1 Clem. 5:4) he suffered a martyr's death c. A.D. 65-67. (For an instructive survey of Peter's preeminence and role in the early church see R. E. Brown, et al., *Peter in the New Testament* listed in the Bibliography.)

The diverse traditions and theological vision contained in 1 Peter are the rich heritage of one whose apostolic mission and sense of God's universal grace took him from one end of the Roman Empire to the other. It is Peter, the "fellow elder, witness to Christ's sufferings, and partaker in the glory to be revealed" (5:1) who is the most vital personal link with the suffering Christians in Asia Minor. Therefore it is in Peter's name that this letter is sent out from the Petrine community in Rome.

1b—"to the elect visiting strangers of the Dispersion in Pontus, Galatia, Cappadocia, Asia, and Bithynia"

These five places locate the addressees in the four Roman provinces of Asia Minor (Bithynia-Pontus formed a single province) north of the Taurus Mountains which spread across southern Asia Minor (present-day Turkey). This vast territory indicates the rapid and extensive spread of Christianity in this predominantly rural and relatively unromanized area of the Mediterranean world. The unusual separation of Pontus from Bithynia may be an indication of the intended route of the letter and its emissaries, commencing at a seaport of Pontus in the east and ending at Bithynia in the west. Whatever the exact route, 1 Peter was in any case designed to be a circular or encyclical communication, addressed not to one particular city (as were Paul's letters) but to a more inclusive area. Since the fourth century, New Testament writings with such a general or even unspecified address were classified together and designated *catholic* (lit. "across the whole land") *epistles* (i.e., James, 1-2 Peter, 1-3 John, Jude).

The term "visiting strangers" here and its combination with "resident aliens" in 2:11 indicates the social condition of the addressees (see Introduction). These strangers or aliens are people who are living temporarily or permanently away from home, who are regarded as socially and culturally inferior to the full citizens and natives, and who as "outsiders" are accorded only limited political, economic, and social rights.

At the outset of the letter, however, these strangers are reminded that as converts to Christianity they have been elected (RSV: **chosen**) by God. This ancient designation of Israel as God's "elect and holy people," with its roots in the sacred covenant formed at Sinai (Exod. 19:3-8), along with other epithets that once applied exclusively to Israel and the Jews such as **Dispersion** or Diaspora (referring originally to Jews "dispersed" from or living outside the Holy Land), the "holy people," the flock or household of God, was expropriated from Judaism by the followers of Jesus to identify the community of Christ as the final and authentic people of God. In 1 Peter the theme of election plays a major role in the reassurance and motivation of its suffering addressees (see esp. 2:4-10). The letter concludes (. . . "co-elect at Babylon," 5:13) as it opens here with a stress on the divine election that unites the faithful strangers in Asia Minor with those in Rome. Although living everywhere as strangers in an alien and hostile environment, Christians may take heart because of God's protective care of his elected ones (5:6-11).

2a—The nature of this election is described according to its origin, mediation, and goal. Christians are elect

• according to the foreknowledge (and hence "plan") of God the Father (see also 1:17),

• through the sanctifying action of the (Holy) Spirit (see also 1:11-12; 4:14 and the role of the Spirit in Christian behavior) and

• for obedience (see 1:14-16, 22; 3:6) and the sprinkling of the (redeeming) blood of Jesus Christ (see 1:19).

Christian election thus originates in the sovereign will and gracious plan of God the Father who gives birth (1:3) to a new community of children or family. It is carried out by the Spirit who maintains the holiness (or set-apartness) of the elect. And election has as its goal an obedience to God's will which is

made possible by the obedience and voluntary death of Jesus
Christ (see 2:18-25; 3:13-22).

2b—The terms **grace and peace** with which the salutation
concludes recur throughout the letter (1:10, 13; 3:7; 4:10; 5:5,
10, 12; 3:11; 5:14, resp.). Like an overture to an opera these
opening verses announce notes and themes that receive fuller
development in the paragraphs that follow.

■ *1:3—2:10   By the mercy of God you strangers in
society have become the elect and holy
people of God, the household of faith.*

This first major section of the letter, bounded by the accent
on God's enlivening mercy (1:3; 2:10), affirms the distinctive
features of corporate Christian identity:
- hope and holiness of life (1:3-5, 13-21),
- joy in suffering as the prelude to salvation (1:6-9),
- experience of the Spirit's good news (1:10-12),
- growth in love and faith (1:22—2:3), and
- election into the household of God the king (2:4-10).

In this section the foundation is laid for the exhortation that
follows in 2:11—5:11.

*1:3-12   Praise be to God for the saving benefits of his
mercy!*

The letter opens, as it closes (5:10-11), with a blessing or
benediction. This suggests the influence of synagogue worship,
which also began and ended with benedictions. For similar
liturgical introductions, perhaps indicating the expected reading of the letter during the public worship, compare the first
words of 1 Peter 1:3 with exactly the same phrasing in 2 Corinthians 1:3 and Ephesians 1:3. The section is composed of three
units echoing the three-part structure of v 2 and its subjects
(God the Father, 3-5; Jesus Christ, 6-9; and Holy Spirit, 10-12).

3-5—*Through the resurrection of Jesus Christ God the Father has given us new birth to a living hope, an imperishable inheritance, and a sure salvation in this final age.*

In Christian baptismal tradition the image of rebirth (1:3, 23; 2:2; Titus 3:5-7; John 3:1-8) or adoption as the children of God (Rom. 8:14-25; Gal. 3:23—4:7) symbolized the effects and implications of conversion to the Christian faith. In baptism the convert totally renounced his former way of life (see 1:17-19; 2:1, 11, 24; 4:1-3), embraced the God of Jesus Christ as Father (1:14-17) and became a member of the household of God (2:5; 4:17), the brotherhood of faith (2:17; 5:9). The threefold results of such a rebirth, according to 1 Peter, are

(1) **a living hope** made possible through God's raising Jesus from the dead (1:3, 21; 2:4; 3:18-22)

(2) **an inheritance** secure in heaven and not linked to any plot of soil like the holy and yet profaned Land of Israel (v 4), and

(3) **a salvation** now about to be revealed in this final age to those who are guarded by God's power (v 5).

The Greek term rendered **guarded** is a picturesque expression for God's protection of his children related to actual conditions of life in these frontier provinces where local rulers and later the Roman army used fortresses to guard the countryside from attack.

6-9—*You can rejoice in this fact and await the revelation of this salvation with love and a faith tested by suffering.*

Continuing the focus on faith and imminent salvation, these verses affirm that the prospect of future exaltation is cause for present exultation. The fact that v 6 introduces suffering as a *possibility*, whereas in 4:12ff. suffering is treated as a *present* reality, has led some commentators to theorize that these different parts of the letter (1:3—4:11, 4:12—5:14) perhaps originated at different times and that 1 Peter in its present form is a combination of previously separate material. The continuity in terminology, style, theme, and structure throughout 1 Peter, however, demonstrate the overall unity of the letter. Illustrative of this unity is also the fact that the present reality of Christian suffering is stressed also prior to 4:12 (e.g., 2:12, 18-20; 3:9, 13-17; 4:1). The sense of 1:6-9 is that even if suffering should become a reality—as later passages indicate was the case—nevertheless there is cause for rejoicing (cf. 2:19 and 4:13).

Such suffering is to be viewed as various trials by which God is "testing" and purifying the genuineness of faith. The process here and in 4:12 (**fiery ordeal,** "test" or **prove**) is compared to the method of refining precious gold through exposing it to the fire (Greek: *pur*) or purification. Such a faith refined by the fire of suffering, and more precious than even gold which perishes, will redound to the believers' praise, glory, and preciousness (rsv: **honor**) **at the revelation of Jesus Christ.** In v 8 love is then also linked with faith and hope (v 4; cf. 1 Cor. 13:13; 1 Thess. 1:3; 5:8) as the characteristic means by which Christians anticipate their salvation.

10-12—*The good news of salvation which the prophets sought has been revealed now exclusively to you.*

These verses link the salvation of the believers to the *expectation* of the prophets but contrast the *experience* of the prophets who represent Judaism with that of the Christians who alone are the actual recipients of God's grace. Indeed, even the angels yearning for a glimpse of this glorious event of the Messiah's coming are not as privileged as *you.* For it was *you* alone that the good news of salvation was preached by those sent to *you* by the Holy Spirit. This personal accent on the "for you" of the gospel is the pastoral and homiletical trademark of this letter. It recalls the similar words of Luther that the good news is not simply news in general but good news *for you, for me.* At the same time adherence to this gospel marks the line of demarcation between the old and the new, the perishable and the imperishable, the redeemed and the unredeemed. Those who hear and heed this word of God are reborn to new life as the children of God (1:23-25). Those, however, who disobey the gospel (4:17) and cause the household of God to suffer shall perish (4:17-19).

The unit as a whole (1:3-12) thus makes clear that to be the *distinctive* and privileged recipients of divine mercy and grace is to be *different* socially as well as religiously. In the following section this combined accent is given further elaboration.

1:13-21 You, God's holy children, are to lead a distinctive, holy way of life indicative of your hope in God's grace.

Beginning with a **Therefore,** 1:13-21 draws the first of a series of ethical consequences from the preceding affirmation of the identity and hope of the reborn children of God (1:3-12). Here **hope** (v 13), linked with **faith** (v 21, as in vv 3, 6-9), is associated with holiness (vv 14-16, 17-20) as key expressions of Christian consciousness and conduct.

The stress on hope which marks the beginning and end of this unit typifies the future-oriented aspect of faith as described in 1 Peter. Such hopeful faith was rooted in the conviction that **the end of all things is at hand** (4:7) because the Christ **who was destined before the foundation of the world** has been manifested at the *end* of all times (1:20). From this Greek word for "end" (*eschatos,* see also 1:5) the term "eschatological" is derived, a term meaning the consciousness of living at the very end of world history. Fulfilling the hopes of the prophets (1:10-12), this Christ in the person of Jesus has liberated and gathered together God's holy endtime community (1:18-19; 2:4-10, 25). His imminent revelation in full glory (1:13;

4:13; 5:1, 4) is the certain signal of the visitation of God (2:12)
who is about to condemn the ungodly and save the righteous
(1:5, 7, 13; 3:21; 4:5-6, 17-19; 5:1).

13—Such an eschatological consciousness involves sober
alertness and resistance to outside pressures to conformity
(1:13; 4:7; 5:8-9). Christians are to await the coming of grace
and salvation with "the loins of their minds girded" (v 13), as
once the Israelites at the first Passover anticipated their re-
demption from Egyptian bondage with girded loins, i.e, with
their robes hitched to their waists and ready for flight (Exod.
12:11).

14-16, 17-20—*Holiness* is to be a hallmark of Christian conduct throughout the time of their residence as aliens. In scriptural tradition "holiness" (lit. "set-apartness"), like election
with which it is frequently joined as in 2:9, has a double connotation. Holy persons are those who are *separated from* the
godless and *united to* God (the "wholly other One"). In its
moral dimension, holiness involves nonconformity to modes of
conduct which are incompatible with the will of God (i.e., the
behavior of the Gentiles, 2:11; 4:1-4) and obedient conformity
to the will of God alone. Having once separated themselves
through conversion from **the passions of your former ignorance**
(1:14) and **the futile ways inherited from your fathers** (1:18),
the Christian converts have been reborn (1:3) into the family
of God and are to be **obedient children** (1:14; see 1:2, 22) of
their new divine Father. As in Jewish piety, God the Holy One
is the model of their holiness (vv 15-16, quoting Lev. 19:2).
Obedience to his will is the measure of their holiness (3:17; 4:2,
19). In addition, however, vv 17-20, as 1:2, make clear the specifically Christocentric *source* of this holiness: ransom/redemp-
tion through **the precious blood of Christ, like that of a lamb
without blemish or spot.**

21—Through this holy Victim raised and glorified by God,
Christian converts now are holy children of a holy heavenly
Father. In their environment they *can* pursue a distinctively

different way of life marked by reverent awe (RSV: **fear;** see 2:17, 19; 3:2, 14, 15) toward their Father and Judge because this sacrifice "for their (your) sake" is the ground of their faith and hope in God.

In 1 Peter, as in the Scripture which it quotes or alludes to (esp. Exod., Lev., Isa.), the concept of holiness (1:2, 14-20; 2:4-10; 3:5, 15) or purity (1:22) is a strategic means for defining the unique character and conduct of God's covenant community. Jewish groups contemporary with early Christianity, notably the Essenes of Qumran, the Pharisees and then rabbinic Judaism as a whole (after A.D. 70) were all claiming to be the one and only holy people of God. The holiness of Christians stressed in 1 Peter is thus to be seen as aimed at demarcating the believers in Jesus Christ from Jews as well as pagans. Only faith in Jesus Christ secures admission to the holy family of God. Faith, regardless of Jewish pedigree or pagan origin, makes this eschatological community open to all people alike.

1:22-25   *As a fraternal community purified through obedience to the truth, maintain your unity through constant familial love; for you have been reborn through the enduring word of the good news.*

This section expands on the communal implications of the preceding themes of holiness ("having purified yourselves"), obedience, and rebirth, and prepares for the unit to follow (2:1-3). The image of the community as the family or household of God is developed through mention of the imperishable seed by which they were reborn and through stress on the love they owe one another as members of God's family.

22-23—Being reborn (1:3) as children of God (1:14) involves relating to other believers as brothers and sisters. Such sincere and unceasing brotherly love is possible because the readers have purified themselves (RSV: their **souls,** i.e., their entire be-

ing) through their **obedience to the truth** (see 5:12, **the true
grace of God**). Their love for each other should not wane or
perish because they have been reborn not from perishable
(human) seed but from **the living and abiding word** (seed) **of
God,** that is, the good news of the Lord which was preached to
them (1:12) and which gave them new life.

24-25—Isaiah 40:6, 8 is cited to substantiate the contrast made
(v 23, as previously in 1:4, 18) between the quality of life before
and after Christian conversion. The wording of the original
Isaiah text is altered ("Lord" is substituted for "our God") to
affirm that the "word" of which the prophet spoke is the very
word concerning the Lord (i.e., Jesus Christ) **which was
preached to you** (v 25, reiterating 1:12).

2:1-3   *Therefore avoid all acts of dissension and continue to feed on the milk of the word, namely, the Lord.*

The contrast between old and new life involves not only
rebirth through the "seed of the word" (1:22-25) but also re-
nunciation of past behavior (2:1) and constant feeding on the
"milk of the word" (2:2-3).

The readers are to **put away** or desist from those Gentile-like
vices (as in 2:11; 4:2-3) which, like **insincerity,** are incompatible
with their purified state of rebirth (cf. James 1:21) and impede
a sincere brotherly love (1:22). Rather than emulating the
slander of their detractors (2:12; 3:16) and their **guile,** they
should long for the guileless milk of the word (RSV: **pure spiritual milk**). As **newborn babes** yearn for mother's milk, so these
newly-born converts should eagerly feed on their "word-milk"
so that they may **grow up to salvation.** Salvation, together with
a living hope and an imperishable inheritance, is the ultimate
goal of Christian regeneration (1:3-5), the outcome of a faith
which remains constant until the Lord's final appearance (1:7-
9, 13). From initial rebirth to final salvation is a process of

growth that requires regular nourishment on the word of
the gospel.

Verse 3 rounds off this image of birth/growth by identifying
the one with whom seed, word, and milk are all linked—Jesus
Christ the Lord. It is his **kindness** which they have already
tasted (echoing Ps. 34:8). At the same time this verse prepares
for the thought that follows: this is the Lord to whom they, as
proselytes to Christianity, have come and continue to come
(in faith).

2:4-10   *Adhere in faith to the Lord Jesus Christ, the Elect*
          and Holy One of God, through whom, by God's
          mercy, you have become the elect and holy com-
          munity of God, the household of the Spirit.

These verses bring the line of thought begun in 1:3 to a re-
sounding climax. By God's great mercy (2:10 echoing 1:3) the
reborn readers (1:3, 23; 2:2) are united by faith with Jesus
Christ (1:6-9, 17-21, 22—2:3); though rejected by men, they too
have been exalted by God. Distinct from all the nonbelievers
who reject Jesus as Lord, they share his holiness (1:14-16, 18-
19, 22) and his election as God's elect and holy people. Reborn
and regathered into a household of the Spirit, they are now to
proclaim through a holy way of life the wonderful saving
deeds of God.

The first major section of 1 Peter (1:3—2:10) thus concludes
with a stirring affirmation of the union of believers with Jesus
Christ and the high privileges and great responsibilities which
are theirs as God's covenant community and household. The
building-blocks of this passage are (1) one set of Old Testament texts cited in vv 6-8 (Isa. 28:16; Ps. 118:22; Isa. 8:14)
concerning a "stone" which in both Jewish and Christian traditions had been viewed as an image of the Messiah (See Mark
12:1-12 par.; Acts 4:8-12; Rom. 9:30-33); (2) another set of
Old Testament texts in vv 9-10 (Exod. 19:6; Isa. 43:20-21;

42:6-9; 63:7-9; Hos. 1:6, 9; 2:1-23) which had once described the great features of God's elect community and family and which now are applied to the endtime people of God; and (3) an introductory pair of verses (4-5) that announce, combine, and apply to both Jesus Christ and believers the sacred epithets which follow (v 4-5a pertaining to vv 6-8 and the rest of v 5 to vv 9-10). Uniting and pervading this complex passage is the ancient covenant theme of divine election (vv 4, 5, 6, 9) which in turn links this passage to a dominant emphasis of the letter as a whole (see 1:1 and 5:13. For a more detailed analysis see John H. Elliott, *The Elect and the Holy*, 1966, in the bibliography.)

4-5a (and **6-8**)—The Lord (referring back to v 3) to whom these converts are coming in faith is a *living* **stone,** i.e., a Messiah who has been *resurrected* by God (see 1:3). Though this Messiah-stone was and is rejected by disbelieving people (vv 4, 7, 8), he is nevertheless *elect* (RSV: **chosen) and precious in God's sight.** Faith in this Messiah-stone distinguishes the readers for whom **he is precious** (v 7) from those who in their disbelief **stumble** over the stone which God has established (v 6, 8) for the salvation of all. Through faith in this **living stone** the believers themselves become **living stones** (5a).

5b (and **9-10**)—Through faith in the *elect stone-Messiah*, believers have become the *elect endtime people of God*. In continuity with ancient Israel and yet distinct from present unbelieving Jews and Gentiles, they now inherit Israel's privileges (vv 9-10) as God's "elect generation" (RSV: **chosen race**) and his *elect covenant community* ("royal dwelling place," "priestly community," "holy nation," and "people" special to God). Their divine calling is now to proclaim publicly his mighty saving deeds. Called from darkness to light, they are like the people of Hosea's time, symbolized by the names and fate of the prophet's illegitimate children. Once they were "Not-my-children" and "Not-shown-mercy." But now God has embraced them and renamed them "People-of-God" and "Those-shown-mercy."

As vv 4-5a selected from and commented on vv 6-8, so v 5b selects from and comments on certain terms of vv 9-10. To create a logical transition from the image of stone to the reality of community, v 5 uses terminology (in Greek) which relates to both stones and human community; namely, "build up" *(oikodomeisthai)* and "house/household" *(oikos,* i.e. something built up). In Greek the text reads: "you yourselves as living stones are being built up [by God]; (you are) a household of the [Holy] Spirit, a holy priestly community." As the expression "holy priestly community" anticipates the terms of Exodus 19:6 quoted in v 9, so "household of the (royal or divine) Spirit" anticipates and interprets the Greek term *basileion* (royal dwelling place) in v 9. Thus the elected people of the covenant, who once formed the kingdom or dwelling place of God, are now declared to be the household or family in whom the King's Spirit resides. Similarly, the activity of God's people described as "to offer sacrifices motivated by the Spirit" in v 5 correlates with and comments on the phrase in v 9: **that you may declare the wonderful** (saving) **deeds of him who called you out of darkness into his marvelous light.**

The theme of divine election here has been derived from Isaiah and especially Exodus 19:5-6, a cardinal Old Testament formulation of the covenant contracted at Sinai between God and the house of Jacob whom God had elected as his special possession. This covenant passage was basic to ancient Israel's self-understanding and is cited in v 9 and commented on in v 5b in order to assert that it is now faith in Jesus the elect Messiah-stone that admits all persons, Jews and Gentiles alike, to the new and final elect and the holy covenant people of God, the house no longer of Jacob but of God's Spirit.

This passage thus constitutes an eloquent conclusion to the first section of the letter which has stressed both the distinctive familial identity and the appropriate fraternal conduct of

God's elect and holy people. Strangers in society though they are, by God's mercy they are nevertheless united in faith, obedience, and love as the household of the Spirit.

For the church of the Reformation this passage has played a special role in its understanding of Christian ministry and, even more important, its stress on the conviction that all baptized believers are equal recipients of the full grace of God. Therefore an additional comment might be appropriate at this point.

In criticism of an exaggerated stress on the superior status and special privileges attributed to the clergy of his day and of the virtual restriction of ministry to an ordained priesthood, Martin Luther appealed to vv 5 and 9 of this text as the biblical basis for a concept of the "general priesthood of all believers." (See, e.g., "The Freedom of a Christian" [1520] in *Luther's Works*, vol. 31; and "To the Christian Nobility" [1520], *ibid.*, vol. 44.) His chief point was that holy baptism makes priests and kings of *all* the faithful and that ministry is *every* believer's divine calling.

Luther's reading of this Petrine text was influenced by the situation of his own day: a debilitating gap between the priesthood and the faithful, a lack of lay responsibility in the church, and his own aim of ecclesial reform. When the passage of 1 Peter is analyzed, on the other hand, within its own first-century literary and historical setting, it reveals a rather different meaning. In this original context it is *election* (of Jesus Christ and his community) rather than priesthood which is principally stressed. A priesthood theme, in fact, is nowhere mentioned in the rest of the letter, in contrast to the dominant theme of election. Moreover, this passage affirms not the *equality* of all believers as individual priests or kings but rather cites *collective terms* (generation, dwelling place, household, priestly community, nation, people) to emphasize the *community and divine favor* of the new covenant people of God. Thus, while Luther's concern for the universal *ministry* of all the faithful and their equal status before God certainly has biblical roots elsewhere in the New Testament, it is clear that the authors of 1 Peter were dealing with different problems and responding with different emphases. Through faith in Jesus, the elect and holy Messiah of God, 1 Peter declares, people who were once estranged from God have become his elect and holy community, a family of the reborn in whom his Spirit dwells.

■ *2:11—4:11 As resident aliens and strangers in society, through obedience to God preserve the distinctiveness and solidarity of your household to the glory of God.*

Having established the unique communal *identity* of those who have been elected, sanctified, and united as brothers and sisters by God's mercy (1:3—2:10), the letter next outlines the God-given responsibilities of the household of God in an alien society. Glorification of God is the note on which this section opens (2:12) and closes (4:11).

2:11-12 As the elect and holy household of faith, live as holy strangers in society so that through your distinctive style of behavior even hostile outsiders (Gentiles) might come to glorify God.

These verses provide a transition from a consideration of *who* the believers are to *how* they are to behave in society and within the brotherhood. As a general formulation of the more specific exhortation to follow (2:13ff.) they describe negatively (v 11) and then positively (v 12) the kind of conduct appropriate for believers who are simultaneously resident aliens and visiting strangers (v 11; cf. 1:1, 17) in society and members of the household of God (2:4-10).

As indicated previously (1:14, 18; 2:1) and repeated later (4:1-6), the holy readers are to maintain a distance from the human desires (RSV: **passions of the flesh**) which typify the **Gentiles** (i.e. the non-believers). Accommodation to the ways of the Gentiles is contrary to the will of God (4:2-5). The conflict between believers and unbelievers, symbolized as a state of war (v 11: cf. 4:1) or as an attack by the Devil himself (5:8-9) is not to be underestimated. The very life (**soul**) of the believers is at stake.

On the other hand, these non-believers are to be resisted not by wrongdoing but rather by **good deeds** and a beautiful way of life which will put the lie to their misinformed (2:15) slander (v 12; also 2:18-20; 3:2, 9, 10-12, 15-18; 4:14-16, 19). The objective of such conduct is not merely the silencing of slander or the cessation of hostility, but the ultimate goal of the Christian mission in the world: the universal glorification of God on the final day of divine visitation. **Glorify** (2:12; 4:11, 16) and **glory** (1:7, 11, 21, 24; 4:11, 13, 14; 5:1, 4, 10) in 1 Peter describe the magnificence and splendor of God and its acknowledgment and enjoyment by those who belong to him. This glorification, according to 1 Peter, marks not only Christian worship but also its conduct and mission.

2:13—3:12   *Be subordinate because of the Lord to every institution created for humankind.*

The nature of the **good conduct** of 2:12 is now made more specific. A traditional pattern of household moral instruction is used here as later in 5:1-5 to clarify respective roles, relationships and responsibilities within the household of God. In Greek and Roman as well as Jewish and Christian culture, the household served as the fundamental unit of human association and the chief model for broader types of social organization (clan, tribe, nation, family of nations). In Judeo-Christian tradition it is with reference to the "house" of Abraham, of Jacob, of Israel, of David, and to the new household of Jesus (e.g. Mark 3:21-35 par.) that the history of salvation was written. The household of God was an appropriate symbol for the Christian community which began through the numerous conversions of households (Luke 19:9; John 4:46-53; Acts 10—11; 16:15, 31-34; 18:8; 1 Cor. 1:14, 16; 16:15) and spread throughout the world. The household or family, that eternal focal point of social identity and spiritual well-being, supplied early Christianity with a powerful set of symbols for the expression of faith (God as father, Jesus as brother, fellow believers as sisters and brothers), and moral responsibility. While several New Testament writings portray the church as a household of faith (Mark 3:21-35 par., Gal. 6:10; Eph. 2:19-21; 1 Tim. 3:5, 15; cf. Titus 1:7; Heb. 3:1-6) or exhort the believers through household codes (Eph. 5:22—6:9; Col. 3:18—4:1; 1 Tim. 2—6; Titus 2—3; 1 John 2:12-14), it is in 1 Peter that the relation of the familial identity and responsibility of the faithful is most clearly emphasized.

In 2:13ff. subordination (RSV: **be subject:** 2:13, 18; 3:1, 5; also 5:5) and "doing good/right" (2:14, 15, 20; 3-6, 17; 4:19) as contrasted to "doing evil/wrong" (2:14, 19; 3:9, 10, 11, 12, 13; 4:15) function as thematic terms for describing appropriate Christian conduct. Order within the household is to be maintained through the willingness to be subordinate. Ultimately all creatures, institutions, and powers are subordinate to God the creator (4:19) and the exalted Christ (3:22). Such subordination, like **doing right,** is submission and obedience to **God's will** (2:15; 3:17; 4:2, 19). To live in accord with this norm alone is to act with a clear conscience (3:16, 21; that is, to be **mindful of** (the will of) **God** (2:19; 5:2).

2:13-17   *Be subordinate to civil authority, but love the brotherhood and fear only God.*

Verse **13** urges subordination to, as the RSV marginal note suggests, **every institution ordained for men by God.** The term translated **institution** literally means "creature" and thereby implies that it is God who as creator ordains human authority and orders human relationships (cf. 4:19). "Because of" or **for the Lord's sake** states briefly the Christological motivation which is described more extensively in 2:21-25. The relation between the household of God and the household of Caesar is described in vv 13b-17 with relative neutrality and restraint. In contrast to Paul's earlier commendation of civil rulers as ministers of God (Rom. 13:1-7) and the prophet John's later condemnation of Roman authorities as agents of the devil (Rev. 13; 17–18), 1 Peter simply recommends Christian subordination to the emperor and his governors in the provinces since their responsibility is to **punish those who do wrong and to praise those who do right** (13b-14).

This neutrality is a significant indication of the date of the letter and of the situation of Christianity within the empire. Following emperor Nero's execution of Christians at Rome for their supposed complicity in the great fire of 64, 1 Peter no longer shares the thoroughly positive assessment of civil authority expressed in Paul's letter to the Romans (c. 57). On the other hand, the Christians of Asia Minor had not yet experienced the tribulations described in the Revelation of John (c. 96). This situates 1 Peter during the relatively peaceful years of Christian-Empire relations, (i.e. c. 70-90 and points to local animosity rather than official Roman "persecution" as the cause of the sufferings mentioned in the letter. The subordination to and respect for the emperor encouraged in 1 Peter would hardly be conceivable, were Christians suffering at the hands of Roman authorities, as Revelation later demonstrates.

15-16 To the local population, the Christians and their God were a strange and unknown quantity. Ignorance, the wellspring of suspicion, fear, prejudice and slander, had to be overcome with righteous action and not just words (as also stressed in 3:1-2). In the culture of the day, only **free men** (v 16) were considered fully human (not owned as chattel by someone else). In the Christian reversal of values, however, real freedom came from being **servants of God,** being owned by God "whose service is perfect freedom." Therefore liberty could never be exploited as the license for evil.

17—Four parallel imperatives summarize this section by contrasting external to internal relationships. Like **all men** (17a), so too **the emperor** deserves **honor** (17d). **Love,** however, is reserved for the **brotherhood** (17b, see 5:9; 1:22; 3:8) just as awe and reverence (RSV: **fear**) is due to God alone (17c; see 1:17; 3:2, 15; cf. 3:6, 14). As in the Lord's words which the Gospels recall (Matt. 22:21/Mark 17:17/Luke 20:25), the Christian readers of 1 Peter also are to render to Caesar [only] what is Caesar's, and to God what is God's.

2:18-20 *Household slaves, be subordinate to your owners by doing good, even if you suffer unjustly.*

From the wider public scene and the civic responsibility of **free men** (v 16), the focus narrows on the household and the calling of Christian household slaves. The servants addressed here were in fact slaves owned by masters. However the Greek term used here *(oiketai)* stresses their place and function within the household *(oikos).* In other New Testament domestic exhortation (Col. 3:18—4:1; 5:22—6:9; 1 Tim. 2:8—6:2; Titus 2:1-10), slaves (and masters) are addressed *last* (indicating their inferior rank on the social ladder). In 1 Peter, however, household slaves are mentioned *first* and through their association with the suffering Lord (2:21-25) are made an example for the entire household of faith.

Household slaves who **endure pain while suffering unjustly,** who suffer though they do good exemplify the predicament of the entire suffering community. Likewise by being **mindful of God** and therefore being subordinate to harsh and unjust as well as gentle masters, they exemplify the vindicating grace of God (RSV: **God's approval,** 19, 20) by which all the faithful are sustained (5:10).

2:21-25 *You (household slaves) have been called to follow*
the Christ who, by also suffering unjustly in subordi-
nation to the will of God, has made it possible for
you to do the same.

21a—The unrelenting doing of good even in the face of undeserved suffering is a cardinal feature of the calling of all those who bear the name of the Christ.

21b-25—Like these servants and all the suffering Christians, Christ also suffered as a servant faithful to God's will and established an **example** of innocence and non-retaliation for all the household to follow. The details of Christ's suffering (vv 22-23) and its saving effects (vv 24-25) form a mosaic drawn from the Passion tradition and composed in accord with the Suffering Servant song of Isaiah 52:13—53:12. This Servant's innocent suffering (22), non-retaliatory (23) and vicarious (**he himself bore our sins. . . . By his wounds you have been healed,** 24) suffering and self-entrustment to God (**him who judges justly,** 23) has brought about a radical change in the lives of the believers.

Sin may be overcome and we can live righteously (see 4:1); his wounds have effected your healing; you wandering sheep have been gathered together by your Shepherd-Guardian (see 5:4 and the shepherd image in John 10:10-18; Heb. 13:20; Rev. 7:17). Christ the Example is Christ the Enabler. Christians can **follow in his steps** (21b) because he has first forged the way. The self-sacrificing suffering of the Servant makes the suffering of the believing servants possible. The sheep which the shepherds tend (5:2) is the flock which the Chief Shepherd has first gathered (2:25; 5:4).

3:1-6 Wives, be subordinate to your husbands by doing good and not fearing them.

1-4—Christian wives likewise are to be subordinate to their non-believing husbands in order that the latter **may be won** (to the faith; see the same missionary sense to the word in 1 Cor. 9:19-22). As in 2:12, it is *action, not words,* which is stressed as the effective means of missionary witness. Subordination consists of pure behavior motivated by reverence (for God); see the comments on 2:13ff. above. Christian winsomeness is not a matter of external cosmetics (from Greek *kosmos,* RSV: **adorning,** 3:3) but a purity of the heart manifested in a gentle and peaceful spirit which God counts **precious** (v 4).

5-6—Sarah's obedience to her husband Abraham (Gen. 18:1-15) illustrates the subordination of the "holy wives" of the patriarchs which the Christian wives are now to emulate. Believers in general were regarded to be the children of Abraham, (Rom. 4:11-12; Gal. 3:7, 16, 29; Heb. 2:16), the father of God's people and first "resident alien" (Acts 7:6; Heb. 11:9). Here it is Abraham's wife, Sarah, who is declared to be the spiritual mother and model of Christian wives who do right and show no fear of any who might oppress them (see 3:14).

3:7 Husbands, live in household harmony with your wives and respect them as co-heirs of the grace of life.

In contrast to the wives addressed in 3:1-6, it is assumed that the husbands of 3:7 have Christian spouses. These husbands are encouraged, literally, to "live in household unity with" *(synoikountes)* their wives by being considerate of their (physical) weakness and by showing them honor because they are co-heirs of the grace of life. In antiquity women were considered inferior to men intellectually and morally as well as physically. The Jewish male gave thanks to God daily that he had not been made a Gentile, a boor, or a woman. 1 Peter,

however, reflects the new and revolutionary Christian consciousness that grace and faith have put an end to previous
modes of sexual as well as social and ethnic discrimination
(Gal. 3:28). In Christian marriages, neither spouse is sole master of the other; the relationship is rather one of mutual respect, (see 1 Cor. 7:3-4). To live together **in Christ** (3:16;
5:10, 14) is to share equally in the **honor** (the same Greek
term is used in 3:7 and 2:7) and grace bestowed through
Christ. This unity of husband and wife assures their unity with
God which is maintained through an unhindered life of prayer
(v 7).

Conduct and prayer, the relationship to other people and to
God, are "horizontal" and "vertical" expressions of the same
reality (see Matt. 5:23-24; 6:12, 14-15; 25:31-46; 1 Cor. 11:20-
29; James 5:9, 13-18; 1 John 4:19-21).

*3:8-12   All members of the household, maintain the unity of
          the community; you have been called to avoid evil
          and do good.*

A general appeal to *all* household members concludes this
section of the letter (2:13—3:12). The one remaining unit concerning subordination (5:1-5a) is reserved for the end of the
letter and is followed by a similar general conclusion (5:5b-7).
The content of vv 8-9 represents the common ethical and catechetical tradition of the early church (cf. Matt. 5:5-7, 43-48;
Luke 6:27-28; Eph. 4:1-3, 32; Col. 3:12-15 and esp. Rom. 12:9-
21 and 1 Thess. 5:13-22). Verses 10-12 are a slightly altered
quotation of Ps. 34:13-17 containing the basic ethical maxim:
"avoid evil and do good."

8—Actions are encouraged here which foster harmony and
cohesion *within* the brotherhood. Christians are to be of one
mind and purpose, sympathetic, (lit. "brother-lovers" *[phila-
delphoi]*, see 1:22; also 2:17; 5:9, 12-14), **of a tender heart and
a humble mind** (as in 5:5b). Humility in particular distinguished

the Christian system of values from that of its secular environment. In the secular world, to be humble was to be base and of no account. For those who lived by the teaching of the Lord, however, the dignity of the humble was an evangelical expression of God's dramatic reversal of priorities (Mark 10:43-45 par.; Matt. 18:4; 23:11-12; Luke 14:11; 18:14).

9—From *outside* the brotherhood the believers are reviled as was their Lord (2:23). As he did not reciprocate, so neither should they. Rather, since they themselves have been called by God to inherit his blessing (1:4; 2:9, 20; 5:10), believers are to invoke the blessing of God upon non-believers.

10-12—Here, as in 1:16, 24; 2:3 (another quotation of Ps. 34:8), 4:18 and 5:5, Scripture is cited to give concluding support to the point made. The stress of this psalm on life (v 10; cf. 3:7; 2:24), peace (v 11; cf. 3:3, 7, 8) and especially "avoiding evil and doing right" (v 11a; cf. 2:13—3:6) make it an appropriate conclusion to the entire section.

3:13—4:6 Distinguish yourselves by doing good, even in the face of outsiders' hostility; God vindicates the righteous.

In this section which continues the ethical theme of doing what is right, the possibility of suffering is reiterated (cf. 1:6), the contrast between the believers and the non-believers (Gentiles) becomes more explicit (3:13-17; 4:1-6), and a Christological basis is given (as in 2:21-25) for the certainty of God's condemnation of the disobedient and his vindication of the righteous (3:18-22).

3:13-17 If you should be caused to suffer by your detractors, let it be only for the doing of good in obedience to God's will.

13-14a—Doing right (good) or wrong (evil) is the theme that marks the beginning and end of this passage (vv 13, 17) and

provides the link with the preceding verses. Since the face of
the Lord is against those that do evil (3:12), who is there to
harm you if you are zealous for what is right? (v 13; cf. v 11).
The fact that Christians were "zealous for what is right" (see
Titus 2:14), however, could lead to the criticism that such zeal
was a kind of fanaticism (like that displayed by the worshipers
of a local Cappadocian goddess Ma-Bellona whom the Romans
dubbed "fanatics"). Therefore if they should suffer for righteousness' sake, they should be assured that they have God's
blessing (see 4:14). 3:14 (and 4:14) echo the Lord's word of
Matthew 5:10: "Blessed are those who are persecuted for righteousness' sake." In 1 Peter (cf. 2:24), as in Matthew (cf. 3:15;
5:20), righteousness is fidelity to the will of God.

14b-16—Verses 14b-15a are an adaptation of Isaiah 8:12-13
where a contrast is drawn between the prophet and his disciples, on the one hand, and their unfaithful countrymen, on the
other. The former are to fear and sanctify the Lord of hosts
whereas the latter fear only their human enemies, the Assyrians
(see 8:1-15). This same passage of Isaiah (8:14) was cited earlier
in 2:8 to make a similar distinction between the obedient and
the disobedient. Here, as in 3:6, the believers are urged not to
fear their human adversaries (since God alone deserves one's
awe and reverence (i.e., "fear," cf. 1:17; 2:17) but rather, literally, to "sanctify the Christ as Lord," an action consistent
with their holiness (cf. 1:2, 15-16, 22; 2:5, 9; 3:5). **In your hearts**
(15a) and **with gentleness and reverence** (15b) repeat the same
attitude encouraged in 3:2-4.

The **defense** (vv 15b-16) which Christians are to make could
conceivably take place before Jewish and pagan tribunals (see
Luke 12:11; 21:14; Acts 25:16; 2 Tim. 4:16). However, the posture of the outsiders who seek an account of **the hope that is in
you** and who abuse (cf. Luke 6:28) and **revile your good behavior in Christ** suggests a more general situation, and the kind
of defense mentioned in 1 Cor. 9:3; 2 Cor. 7:11, and Phil. 1:7,
16. As a strange and unknown sect encountering suspicion and

slander, the Christians in Asia Minor are called upon to set the record straight, especially concerning their extraordinary hope (1:3, 13, 21; 3:5). Believers who act with a clear conscience will be vindicated by the God to whom they are faithful. Non-believers, however, who abuse the faithful will be **put to shame,** that is, will experience God's condemnation (cf. 2:6; 4:5, 17-18). The brief expression **in Christ** (also 5:10, 14) as in Paul's letters, circumscribes the unique basis of Christian unity, conduct, and hope.

17—The final sentence summarizes the main point of this passage which links it to the foregoing and the following units of the letter. It recapitulates the exhortation of 2:15, 20; 3:6, 11, anticipates the content of 4:12-19, and prepares directly for the Christological proclamation of 3:18-22.

3:18-22   Christs, the righteous One, also suffered innocently. His suffering, death, and resurrection-exaltation is the basis of your salvation and vindication.

This significant passage contains problems that have perplexed interpreters for centuries. Similarities of form and content between these verses and other texts concerning Christ's death and resurrection (e.g., Phil. 2:6-11; Col. 1:15-20, and 1 Tim. 3:16) have suggested the presence or influence of an early Christian hymn or creed. The similarities, however, pertain only to vv 18d and 22 and not to the more prosaic and unusual content of vv 19-21. It is more likely, therefore, that, as in 1:19-20 and 2:22-24, particular units of Christological tradition rather than an entire creed or hymn were employed and expanded. This relatively modern issue concerning the form of these verses is accompanied by further questions of longer standing. What were the ancient views regarding the judgment of the world which underlie the events of Christ's journey described here? Who were these "disobedient spirits" and where were they imprisoned? Where and when did Christ "go" and what did he preach? What are the logical and linguistic connections between vv 18-22 and 4:1-6? Is there any relation between these verses and the later (4th cent.) formulations of the Nicene Creed, especially the descent into hell? Concerning v 19 in particular Martin Luther once exclaimed: "This is a strange text and certainly a more obscure passage than any other passage in the New Testament. I still do not know for sure what the apostle means" (*Luther's Works* Vol. 30, p. 113).

However profound and persistent his uncertainty concerning this text, Luther was surely correct on one major point. The "going" and "preaching" of Christ are related not to his death or to his descent into hell but to his resurrection and ascent into heaven. "Christ ascended into heaven and preached to the spirits . . ." (ibid., p. 115). Further clarification of the conceptual background of these verses is made possible through the comparison of this text with other Jewish and Christian texts of the same period. (For a detailed discussion see William J. Dalton, *Christ's Proclamation to the Spirits* listed in the Bibliography.) In general this passage declares to oppressed Christians in Asia Minor the cosmic extent and ethical implications of their suffering Lord's resurrection and exaltation.

18—That Christ **died for sins** was a traditional formulation of the Christian kerygma (Rom. 5:6, 8; 14:15; 1 Cor. 15:3; 2 Cor. 5:14-15; 1 Thess. 5:10). But the RSV marginal reading, **suffered,** is probably the original term here because of the letter's general focus on suffering as well as its stress in the immediate context. It is innocent suffering that links the believers with their suffering Lord (3:18; 4:1; cf. 4:13; 5:1). Christ suffered, as stated in 2:22-24 with reference to Isa. 52-53, as God's servant, the "righteous one" who "bore the sins of many" (Isa. 53:11f., cf. 2 Cor. 5:21, 1 Peter 2:24). **That he might bring us to God** implies that the previously unrighteous now have direct access to God's grace (see Rom. 5:2; Eph. 2:18; 3:12; 1 Peter 5:12). Union with God through removal of the barrier of sin is made possible through Christ's resurrection-exaltation to God's right hand (vv 18, 22). **Put to death in (the) flesh,** that is, in respect to his mortal human existence, he was **made alive** (see "living," 2:4) **in (the) spirit,** that is, in respect to the divine Spirit who gives life (see John 5:21; 6:63; Rom. 4:17; 8:11; 1 Cor. 15:22. For this traditional contrast of flesh and spirit designating human vs. divine, death-determined vs. life-determined existence see also Rom. 1:3-4; 8:1-17, and 1 Tim. 3:16).

19-21—**Made alive in (the) spirit** (v 18d) and **who has gone into heaven** (v 22) refer to the resurrection-exaltation of Christ and circumscribe the occasion of the events related in vv 19-21. These verses are introduced between vv 18 and 22 in order to describe the implications of **the resurrection of Jesus Christ** (v 21) for the disobedient, on the one hand, and for the righteous on the other. As the resurrection of Christ and its proclamation inaugurates a demarcation between old and new life (1:3), sinful and righteous behavior (2:24; 4:1-2), so it also distinguishes the condition of the disobedient from that of the faithful (stumbling and honor, 2:7-8; shame and blessing, 3:16, 14; condemnation and salvation, 4:5-6, 17-18). Here, likewise, a lesson is drawn from the contrast between the "disobedient spirits" and righteous Noah, a lesson from "first time" which is to serve the people in "end time."

Jewish and Christian literature of the period amply demonstrates how the conviction that the end of the world was at hand prompted speculation concerning the beginning of the world. For the events of primordial history were considered a prototype of the manner in which history would end. Among other equations of primordial time and end time, the period of the flood figured prominently. In order to affirm the certainty of divine judgment and the need for righteousness in the present, much attention was given to the original introduction of wickedness and sin into the world. This occurred, it was said, through the agency of disobedient angelic spirits whose lustful impregnation of human women created giants and who in turn were eternally imprisoned by God. Then God destroyed this wicked humanity—with the exception of Noah and his family—through the flood (all elaborations on Gen. 6-7; see e.g., Sirach 16:7; Wisdom 14:6-7; 3 Maccabees 2:4, Jubilees 5; Baruch 3:26-27; Matt. 24:37-39; Luke 17:26-27; Heb. 11:7; 2 Peter 2:4-5; Jude 6).

It is in relation to this apocalyptic tradition, particularly illustrated in the book of 1 Enoch, that this passage of 1 Peter is best understood. According to this widely influential writing, the mysteries of the future were revealed in a series of dream-visions to Enoch, a righteous man whom God took to himself (cf. Gen. 5:21-24). In these visions Enoch ascended from earth and "went" through a series of heavens where he announced to the angelic spirits of the flood age who were imprisoned there that as a result of their wickedness they would be perpetually bound in prison (1 Enoch 6-11 records the fall of the angels and their imprisonment; chapts. 12-21, Enoch's proclamation).

1 Peter 3:19-20 depicts the resurrected Christ as an "end time Enoch" who, like his righteous predecessor, heralded (rsv: **preached,** v 19) God's power and judgment over these same "disobedient spirits." These spirits were imprisoned (by God) not below the earth (in hades/hell) but above the earth in the heavenly realms. Thus the image is that Christ, as he was raised to life (v 18) and passed through the heavens in order to be exalted at God's right hand (v 22), announced the perpetual condemnation of these spirits and their subordination to him (**with angels, authorities, and powers subject to him,** v 22).

Likewise in vv 20-21, as in 1 Enoch 10:1-3; 65-67; 106:15-18; 107:3), righteous Noah and his family (including his wife, three sons and their wives) prefigure the divine salvation of the faithful minority amid the destruction of the whole world. As God once saved while he destroyed with the deluge, so now in the present a believing minority again is being saved through the deluge of its baptism. This baptism, however, is not simply an external removal of the body's dirt but an internal and con-

tinual pledge of (rather than RSV **appeal to**) a clear conscience
to God. Baptism, which has introduced the believers to the new
life inaugurated by the resurrection of Christ (1:3), now saves
by fostering steadfast commitment to God's will (see 2:19; 3:16).

22—This verse completes the unit on Christ's death and resurrection and makes clear that the journey of the resurrected
Christ through the heavens was the occasion of his preaching
mentioned earlier (the same Greek term, *poreutheis*, "having
gone" is used in both vv 18 and 22). As in other Christian inter-
pretations of Christ's resurrection, the subordination of the
angels (including the disobedient angelic spirits), authorities,
and powers declares the universal (earth and heaven) extent
of God's power and reign through Christ (Matt. 28:18-20; 1
Cor. 15:20-28; Eph. 1:20-23; Phil. 2:9-11; Col. 2:20). In 1 Peter
this forms the Christological basis for the subordination of the
faithful (2:13ff.) as well as for their assurance in 4:5, 17-18
that the disobedient non-believers who currently oppress the
faithful will, like the disobedient spirits, be judged by God.

*4:1-6   Separate yourselves from the sinful outsiders who con-
demn you. God will condemn them and vindicate the
faithful.*

Returning to the situation of confrontation between believers and non-believers (3:13-17), this section draws implications
(**Since therefore,** 4:1) from Christ's suffering and resurrection
for the present conduct of converted Christians. The suffering
Christians are compared with the suffering Christ (4:1) and
contrasted to the sinful outsiders (**Gentiles**) who oppose God
and his people (vv 2-4). In the final judgment the tables will be
turned. The ungodly who now condemn will themselves be
condemned and the faithful who are now condemned will be
made alive (vv 5-6).

1—To **suffer in the flesh** (i.e., physically), as Christ suffered
(i.e., **for doing right,** 3:17, 18), is a means for making a break

from sin and battling against it. In the "war" against sin (recalling 2:11), believers are to arm themselves with the memory of
Christ's suffering and to "cease from sin" by "dying to sin" (see
2:21-24); that is, allowing sin no power over their lives. (For
the armor by which believers are to defend themselves against
the unbelievers, see Rom. 13:12; 2 Cor. 6:7; 10:4; Eph. 6:11-17;
1 Thess. 5:8).

2-4—To **cease** (or make a break) **from sin** requires not only
separating oneself from sinful human desires (RSV: **passions**) but
also from the company of the sinful. Conversion and fidelity to
the will of God requires rejection of the ways of the **Gentiles.**
During the remainder of their physical life (v 2) as strangers
in society, the now holy children of God (1:14-16) are to manifest their having been **ransomed from the futile ways inherited
from your fathers** (1:18) by letting **the time that is past** (i.e., the
time prior to their conversion) **suffice for doing what the Gentiles like to do** (v 3a).

The list of prohibited vices (cf. 2:1; 3:9; 4:15) illustrates here
as elsewhere in the New Testament the types of conduct which
Christians considered incompatible with **the will of God** (cf.
Mark 7:21-22; Rom. 1:29-31; 13:13; 1 Cor. 5:10-11; 6:9-10; 2
Cor. 12:20-21; Gal. 5:19-21; Eph. 5:3-5, 18; 1 Tim. 1:9-10; 2 Tim.
3:2-5; Titus 3:3; Rev. 21:8; 22:15). Drunkenness, revels and
carousing in particular were associated with the banquets held
by the numerous trade guilds and social clubs in Asia Minor.
Although the readers may once have held membership in such
guilds and associations for the economic as well as social ad-
vantages they offered especially to strangers and foreigners,
the religious dimensions of such associations (like the guild of
Dionysian artisans with its worship of Dionysus) now made the
continued participation of the Christian converts impossible.
For those who have been sanctified and made the children of
God such activity constituted **lawless idolatry** and a flood of
dissipation (RSV: **wild profligacy**). In withdrawing from such
entangling alliances the Christians have incurred the surprise

and then the scorn of their erstwhile cronies who blaspheme
(RSV: **abuse**) both the Christians and the God whom they
worship.

5-6—But, the letter assures its readers, such nonconformity
has its divine reward. According to God's gracious reversal of
values and destinies, the very ones who now **call you to account**
(3:15) will (on the day of judgment) themselves have to **give
account to him who is ready to judge the living and the dead**
(a fixed expression for *all* creatures, see Acts 10:42 [Peter's
words], Rom. 14:9; 2 Tim. 4:1). Among these **dead** were some
to whom the good news was preached but who had since died,
as in the situation reflected in 1 Thess. 4:13-18. This preaching
and their faith, however, was not in vain, for God's power
extends over all. Even though by human reckoning they seem
condemned physically (because they were dead and presum-
ably therefore not saved), according to God's reckoning they
shall, like the Christ (3:18), live in the realm of the Spirit (v 6).
Sustaining all the contrasts between believers and non-believers and the urgency of a distinctive Christian morality (3:13–
4:6), is the believers' firm hope in the vindicating power of God
and their share in the life of their Lord.

4:7-11   *Maintain the solidarity of the household of God to the glory of God.*

Here the familiar theme of internal familial unity is again
emphasized. Maintenance of communal cohesion and support
was absolutely necessary if Christians were to resist the en-
croachments of their environment (3:17–4:6; 4:12-19; 5:8-9) and
give a concerted witness to the glory of God. A comprehensive
stress on **all things** (v 7) and **everything** (v 11) frame this unit
which concludes the exhortation of 2:11–4:11.

7—**The end of all things is at hand; therefore** . . . . As elsewhere in the letter, and generally in the New Testament, an
eschatological consciousness is the motivation of a Christian

ethic (see the commentary on 1:13-21; cf. also Matt. 24-25; Mark 13; John 13-17; Rom. 13:11-14; Heb. 10:25; 1 John 2:28-29). Being mentally alert and self-controlled (RSV: **sane and sober;** in contrast to the dissipations of 4:3) was essential not only for effective prayer (see Mark 14:38) but also for the resistance to evil (1:13-16; 5:8-9) and communal harmony (4:7-11).

8—The unfailing maintenance of love for one another was of paramount (**above all**) importance because this was the tie that bound together the brotherhood (1:22; 2:17; 3:8; 5:14). That **love covers a multitude of sins,** while apparently influenced by Prov. 10:12 (see also James 5:20), is best understood in the light of Ps. 32:1: "Blessed is he whose transgression is forgiven, whose sin is covered." The Old Testament expression "to cover" was synonymous with the term "to forgive." As God through his love has covered (forgiven) your sins, so now you are to cover (forgive) the sins of your brothers and sisters (cf. 1 Cor. 13:7). For the link between both acts of forgiveness see Matt. 6:12/Luke 11:4; Matt. 18:21-35; Luke 7:47.

9—Extending hospitality, a household-to-household enterprise, was another essential means for consolidating the household of God. The provision of shelter and economic as well as social support to traveling Christians was basic to the mission and expansion of the early Christian movement. If this was the case for the relatively confined area of Galilee (see Matt. 10:10-15 par.), it was all the more imperative for the Christians dispersed throughout the vast region of Asia Minor.

The qualification ungrudgingly recognizes that hospitality could also be regarded as a burden as in the situation of 3 John. However, the association of (brotherly) love and hospitality in vv 8 and 9 (as in Rom. 12:9-13 and Heb. 13:1-2), makes clear that the latter was nothing less than a practical expression of the former.

10-11—Members of the household of God have each received a divine gift (charisma) by which they are to serve one another, thereby strengthening the community and glorifying God.

Each divine gift is a particular manifestation of **God's varied grace** *(charis*—the same Greek root; cf. 3:7). Stress upon these divine gifts as a means of mutual ministry is similar to that in Paul (Rom. 12:6-8; 1 Cor. 12:4-11; cf. Eph. 4:7, 11-12). Whereas for Paul, however, the image for the church within which these gifts are exercised is that of the "body of Christ," in 1 Peter the controlling image of community is that of the household. Accordingly, the believers are described as **good** (household) **stewards of God's varied grace.** A household steward *(oikonomos)* managed the practical affairs of his master's property or household *(oikos)*. Here and elsewhere in the New Testament, the term is used metaphorically to describe those who serve in the household of God (e.g., Luke 12:42-48; 16:1-8; 1 Cor. 4:1-2; Titus 1:7).

Whoever speaks . . . **whoever renders service** (v 11) reflects the traditional division of Christian tasks into word and deed (Acts 6:1-6; Rom. 15:18; 2 Thess. 2:17; Col. 3:17). All gifts come from God. He or she whose gift is to speak (preach, prophesy, teach) utters words (RSV **oracles**) which God has inspired. He or she who ministers or renders service *(diakoneo),* should do so recognizing that it is God who supplies the strength for this task.

This second major section of the letter concludes, as it opened (2:12) on a doxological note. Mutual service within the household of God, like all Christian conduct in society, has as its ultimate goal the glorification of God. The doxological formula itself (**to him belong glory** . . .) and the **Amen,** by which such benedictions are normally accompanied, mark off a major section of the letter (2:11–4:11) rather than indicate the termination of some hypothetical source. Verse 11 is not the conclusion of some independent piece incorporated in 1:3–4:11 (a baptismal homily, liturgy, or separate letter) as has often been proposed. It is rather a pause, or better a punctuation of glory, that also prepares for what immediately follows (4:12-19). The

glory which is God's is also the glory that rests upon suffering
Christians (4:14).

■ *4:12-19   Rejoice in the test which your suffering
             brings for being God's distinctive house-
             hold.*

At this point the crescendo of familiar themes (suffering and
joy, glorification, distinction of the righteous household from
unrighteous outsiders, doing right, and subordination to God)
reaches a high point. The integration of these themes within
the eschatological scope of God's presence and judgment provides a powerful rationale for the maintenance of Christian
integrity, solidarity, and hope. In addition to the continuity of
theme, the structure of this major unit also resembles other
passages of the letter. For the sequence of (a) general statement (vv 12-13), (b) specific negative and then positive illustration (vv 14-16), and (c) substantiating and integrating conclusion (vv 17-19) see 1:13-16, 17-21, 22-25; 2:1-3, 11-12, 13-17,
18-20; 3:1-6, 8-9, 13-17; 4:1-6; 5:1-4.

12-13—Beginning once again (cf. 2:11) on the note of love
(**Beloved**) that binds recipients and senders of the letter (cf.
also 5:14), these verses affirm that suffering is not a reason for
surprise but a sign of solidarity. The element of surprise with
its connotation of estrangement fits the situation of social alienation and relates to the condition described in 4:4. Former Gentile cronies feel surprised and estranged from believers who
have broken their social ties. Reproach and suffering is the
result. This estrangement and the suffering it incurs should
not strike the believers as something **strange** (from the same
Greek root as the verb) to their Christian experience because
this is a sign of their **share** in **Christ's sufferings.** Moreover,
through this **fiery ordeal** of suffering, God is testing or proving
their faith. (For this same constellation of terms and imagery

for the purification and testing of faith through the fire of suffering see 1:6-7 and its commentary.) To share in Christ's sufferings now is, therefore, grounds for present joy, a joy which will be complete when present sufferers also share in his glory soon to be revealed (cf. 1:8-9).

14-16—Two grounds for suffering are contrasted: suffering reproach **for the name of Christ** (v 14) or **as a Christian** (v 16) over against suffering for disobeying God's will (v 15). These verses are among the most crucial in 1 Peter for determining the historical situation of the letter as a whole. The combination of suffering **for the name of Christ** with suffering as a **murderer or a thief** could suggest that merely being a Christian and bearing that name was a criminal offense punishable by Roman law. In this case the sufferings to which 1 Peter refers would be the result of an official Roman policy of prosecution and persecution of the Christian church.

Such a theory, although often advanced, is extremely weak. From the first two centuries there is no evidence of such an official Roman position regarding the Christian movement. In their sporadic dealing with Christians, provincial administrators such as Pliny, the governor of Bithynia-Pontus, required specific instructions from the emperor in lieu of such a general policy (see the Pliny-Trajan correspondence, ca. A.D. 111/112 in Bettenson, ed. *Documents of the Christian Church*, pp. 5-7). Moreover, the very general and non-juridical terms **wrongdoer** and **mischief-maker** in v 15, as well as the continuing stress on God's will as the chief criterion of Christian conduct (v 19; cf. 2:15, 19; 3:16-17; 4:2), suggest that v 16 refers to violations of God's will, not of Roman law. In these verses, as in 2:11-12, 18-20; 3:13-17; 4:1-6, a contrast is made between behaving as a Christian obedient to God and behaving as a Gentile estranged from God. The suffering that resulted from such exclusive fidelity was not instigated by Roman persecution but by popular local resentment.

Such hostility was bred by a combination of factors. It was

the manifestation of conventional native resistance to any social or religious movement representing something strange or new. Local ignorance regarding the Christians (2:15; 3:15) bred suspicion that these strangers were up to no good, or were evil-doers (2:12, 14; 4:15). Confusion of the Christians with Jews and with other exotic Eastern cults or unapproved social clubs prompted the assumption of guilt by association.

Verses 14-16 therefore urge that a clear distinction be made between the conduct appropriate and inappropriate to the household of God. The terms of v 15 recall in general the prohibitions of the second table of the Decalogue which served as a basis for Christian as well as Jewish morality (see Mark 10:17-22 par.; Rom. 13:9; 1 Cor. 5:10-11; 6:9-10; Eph. 6:1-3; James 2:8-13; Rev. 22:15). **Wrongdoer** is the literal contrast to "obeyer of God's will," that is, "gooddoer" (as in 2:12, 14-15; cf. 3:11).

Mischief-maker (Greek *allotriepiskopos*) occurs only here in the New Testament and nowhere in secular Greek. Its component parts in Greek suggest that the term refers to someone who makes himself an "overseer" of the affairs of "others" with whom he has no natural affiliation and for whom he has no responsibility. Here, where the context stresses **the household of God** (v 17), the term was probably used to discourage Christians from meddling in the affairs of outsiders beyond the pale of the community; see 1 Cor. 5:12-13 for a similar restriction.

Verses 14 and 16 parallel each other and express the positive contrast to the prohibitions of v 15. A "Christ-ian" is one who is pledged to the Christ. In antiquity a person's name was regarded as an expression and determination of his/her personality, familial and group identity, and even destiny. Abraham ("father of a multitude of nations," Gen. 17:5), like Jesus ("God saves," Matt. 1:21) and Christ ("anointed one of God,") are more than individual labels or titles. These names identify the persons and events through which the history of salvation has been shaped, new communities created, and hope articulated. The followers of Jesus the Christ preached, healed, and baptized in his name (Mark 9:37-41; Acts 2:21, 38; 3:6, 16; 4:12, 17-18, 30; 5:28); in his name they also suffered (Acts 5:41; 9:16). The joy (v 13; cf. 1:6-9) and blessing (v 14; cf. 3:14) that accompanied **reproach for the name of Christ** recall the Lord's own word of blessing (Matt. 5:11-12/Luke 6:22) and the suffering "for my name's sake" of which he spoke (Mark 13:13 par.; Luke 21:12). Allegiance to the name of Christ Jesus and the conflicts this brought about were the marks of discipleship from the outset.

The term **Christian,** on the other hand, was not a self-designation chosen by the believing community which saw itself rather as the Israel of God (Gal. 6:16) or God's elect and holy people (1 Peter 2:9). The Latin formation of the term "Christian" (from *Christianus*) and its first use in Syrian Antioch (Acts 11:26; see 26:28), together with its non-occurrence anywhere else in the New Testament, indicate that it was first applied to followers of Jesus Christ by Latin-speaking pagans. It was used in a derogatory sense to ridicule these Jewish sectarians infatuated with their Christ as "Christ-lackeys," similar to the term by which many Romans scorned the ridiculous partisans of the emperor Nero (compare *Christiani* and *Augustiani*, devotees of Nero who claimed to be Augustus reincarnate).

According to 1 Peter, however, "man proposes but God disposes." What humans consider shameful, God regards as glorious. The supposed name of scorn is the very name by which God is glorified. Those who would impute shame to the Christians will themselves be put to shame (2:6; 3:16).

17-19—The judgment theme and the future of those inside and outside the **household of God** here becomes explicit. The lines of demarcation are clear and judgment is imminent. Obedience to **the gospel of God,** innocent suffering for fidelity to God's will and "doing right" distinguish the household of believers who are one with the Christ and will share in his glory, from the disobedient, the impious and the sinners who now scorn the household and cause it to suffer. They ultimately stand condemned (4:5). If the righteous who are being saved suffer now, imagine the final lot of the ungodly! (v 18 quoting Prov. 11:31 Greek). The final verse (17) summarizes the heart of the exhortation from 2:11 onward and concludes on a note of consolation. The Procreator of the household (see 1:3, 23) is also Creator of the world (see 2:13; for the combination of Father and Creator see 1 Clem. 62:2). **Those who suffer according to God's will** may entrust themselves to the care of their faithful (Pro)creator (cf. 5:6-7).

In this section (4:12-19), as in 2:4-10, the believing community is expressly called the household of God (4:17; cf. a spiritual house in 2:5). The solidarity of the faithful stressed in 2:4-10—especially their union with God, Christ, and one another—reappears in 4:12-19 as the basis and motive for their endurance of suffering. Suffering Christians who obey the God of the household (vv 16-19) share not only the **name** (vv 14, 16) but also the **sufferings** and the **glory** (v 13) of the Christ. Proved and approved by God (v 12), they experience his glorious presence (v 14). Therefore suffering is cause not for despair or defection but joy and blessing (vv 13, 14). By suffering for doing good, Christians give glory to God (v 16). The God by whom the family of the faithful was called into being is the one who in their suffering now sustains them.

■ *5:1-11   Maintain the unity of the household of God, resist the forces of evil, and commit yourselves to the care of God.*

The combination of encouragement and exhortation that marks 1 Peter throughout is the double note on which the body of the letter ends. The exhortation to leaders (1-4), recent converts (5a) and all the faithful (5b-9) to foster the harmony of the household in order to oppose the forces of evil with a united front (8-9) is undergirded with the encouragement that the God to whose care they commit themselves (6-7) is the one whose power and grace will strengthen them (10-11). An appeal to Christian leaders (**elders**) and recent converts (**you that are younger,** v 5a), that is, to the most senior and most junior members of the household of God, completes the scheme of household instruction employed earlier in 2:13—3:7. Here (vv 5b-6), as earlier (3:8-9), the exhortation concludes with a stress on the mutual respect and spirit of humility required of "all" the believers. Verses 6-11 build on this theme of humility and relate it to the power of God (RSV: mighty hand of God, v 6; **dominion,** v 11) on which note these final verses begin and end.

5:1-4　*Leaders, be responsible and not selfish shepherds of God's flock.*

Reference to one last set of roles, relationships, and responsibilities within the household of God (the theme of 2:13—3:7) has been reserved until this point in the letter in order to emphasize further details of the bond that unites its recipients and senders. The very experiences of the recipients, sharing in Christ's sufferings and glory (4:13), were those experienced by the one in whose name this letter was written. Peter, too, through his death as well as his life was **a witness of the sufferings of Christ as well as a partaker** ("sharer") **in the glory that is to be revealed** (v 1). In addition to this experiential bond he was a **fellow elder.** This unique term found nowhere else in secular or biblical Greek expresses not the uniqueness of Peter as an apostle but rather the common bond through which the elders might be addressed as equals.

On the basis of this bond of shared experience and responsibility the elders are enjoined (vv 2-4) to **tend** ("shepherd") **the flock of God** mindful of their relation to Christ, the **Chief Shepherd** (another term occurring only here in the New Testament but echoing the image of 2:25). An **elder** (rendering the Greek *presbyteros* from which the word "priest" as well as the transliteration "presbyter" derive) originally denoted one who was a senior in age and therefore one to whom responsibility in the community was entrusted. Eventually the term became a title for leaders in Christian as well as Jewish and secular circles regardless of their physical age (e.g., Acts 11:30; 14:23; 1 Tim. 5:17-19; Titus 1:5; 2 John 1; 3 John 1). The function of elders was associated with the task of **exercising the oversight** (*episkopountes* [RSV marginal note, v 2]) such as that exercised by shepherds (in Latin, *pastores*). The combination of terms and images used here and elsewhere in the early church (John 21:15-17; Acts 20: 17-35; Eph. 4:11; 1 Clement 44, 54) provides the language with which Christian community (family, flock) and in particular its pastoral ministry (elders, bishops *[episkopoi]*, and pastors) have ever since been described.

Since the flock is God's, not theirs, shepherds are to tend it because they are willing and eager to serve God's will (v 2), and not because of a shameful desire for financial reward, the well-known motive among non-believers. (For similar warnings against such motives see 1 Tim. 3:3; 6:10; 2 Tim. 3:2; Titus 1:7, 11; Heb. 13:5). Nor should they attempt to lord it over those whom God has given to their care but rather lead his flock by infectious **example** (v 3). The same example of self-giving service that Christ set for all to follow (2:21-25; cf. Mark 10:42-45 par.) is the pattern of life for all elders and shepherds (see also 1 Cor. 10:32—11:1; Phil. 3:17; 1 Thess. 1:5-7; 2 Thess. 3:9). As faithful under-shepherds of the **Chief Shepherd** they too, like Peter, will **obtain the unfading crown of glory** (v 4; cf. v 1).

5:5a   *Recent converts, be subordinate to your leaders.*

Younger is the natural counterpart to "elder." The terms often occur together to contrast age groups (e.g., 1 Tim. 5:1, 2; Titus 2:2, 6). Inasmuch as **elders** in the preceding verses is a

designation of function and not simply age, it is probable that
you that are younger also refers to something other than the
physical age of those addressed. Christian leaders were chosen
from the "first-fruits" or earliest converts to the faith (1 Cor.
16:15-16). They were not to be recent converts (1 Tim. 3:6) but
mature and experienced in the faith. Such a distinction is likely
here. In the household of God recent converts, that is, those
who are young in the faith, should be subordinate to their leaders as children are to parents in the natural family (cf. Eph.
6:1-3).

5:5b-11   *All of you, be humble with one another and be-*
fore God. Be firm in your resistance to evil. The
power of God that exalts you will also confirm
you.

The finale of the letter concerns all the addressees and their
relationship to one another, to God, to the devilish adversary,
and to the worldwide brotherhood. Humility toward one another and God fosters harmony *within* the community (vv 5-7).
Alertness and vigilance are necessary for resisting the threats
to faith from *without* (vv 8-9). Those who remain steadfast in
suffering God will sustain (vv 10-11).

5b-7—Here, as in 3:8, exhortation concerning subordination
(2:13—3:7; 5:1-5a) is balanced by the reminder that humility
is the proper posture of *all* members of God's family. As Christ
suffered and died as God's humble servant (2:21-25; see Phil.
2:5-8), so Christians are to follow in his footsteps. The humility
they practice toward one another is a sign of their common
humility before God. That **God opposes the proud but gives
grace to the humble** is a commonplace of Jewish and Christian
wisdom (Job 22:29; Prov. 3:34; James 4:6). But the picturesque
expression **clothe yourselves . . . with humility** is strikingly
similar to Jesus' humbly clothing himself with a towel to wash
his disciples' feet as an example of mutual respect (John 13:2-

16). Likewise vv 6-7 echo the Lord's instruction regarding self-humbling and divine exaltation (Matt. 23:12; Luke 14:11; 18:14; James 4:10) and entrusting oneself to the fatherly care of God (Matt. 6:25-30).

8-9—As many other passages of 1 Peter have been received into the tradition of the church's worship, especially the hymns, confessions, benedictions, and doxologies which reflected the liturgical life of the early Christians, so these verses have long served as the traditional lesson in the office of Compline, the church's prayer at the close of day. Here at the close of the letter these words encourage believers to resist the devilish adversary with the aid of God's mighty hand (v 6). Pictured as a hungry **roaring lion** (an image for those who threaten God's people, as in Ps. 22:13, 21; Jer. 50:17; Amos 3:12; 3 Macc. 6:7; 2 Tim. 4:17), **the devil** (lit. "the slanderer") symbolizes the evil power behind all those non-believers who oppose God and slander his people (see 2:11-12; 3:13-17; 4:2-5, 12-19; cf. 2 Cor. 4:4; Eph. 6:11-18; James 4:7). The Gentiles, in other words, are in league with the devil. Suffering Christians must resist this common enemy because they are of the family of God. Suffering unites the Christians of Asia Minor not only with Christ and God (4:1-2, 12-19) but also with the entire suffering **brotherhood** (see 2:17) **throughout the world,** including Rome (5:1, 13).

10-11—In this final benediction and doxology of the letter a combination of verbal repetitions give its thought unity and balance. The God who **gives grace to the humble** (v 5b) is **the God of all grace who has called you to his eternal glory in Christ** (v 10). The firmness of faith which believers require (v 9) will be provided by the God who will **restore,** confirm (RSV: **establish**), **and strengthen** them (v. 10). He whose **mighty hand** exalts them (v 6) has the might (RSV: **dominion**) forever (v 11). The duration of suffering will be but a **little while** (v 10 echoing 1:6), for the Lord is soon to appear (1:13). And then his glory (1:11, 21) will be the glory of all who are in **Christ.** The body of the letter thus concludes, as it began, on a note of blessing (1:3; 5:11) and glory (1:7, 8, 11; 5:10) celebrating God's initial (1:3-5) and his final (5:10-11) act of salvation, the commencement and goal of Christian hope.

5:12-14 Conclusion and fraternal greetings

The conclusion succinctly states the purpose of the letter, names the persons involved in its composition and dispatch, and extends greetings, so to speak, "from our part of the household to yours."

The letter was designed as an exhortation (repeating the Greek verb *parakaleo* in 2:11 and 5:1) and witness (see 5:1) concerning **the true grace of God** in which the estranged believers were to **stand fast** (v 12b). This grace of God marks their distinctive identity as God's people (1:10; 5:10), the object of their hope (1:2, 13) and the basis of their conduct within the household of God (3:7; 4:10; 5:5).

Included among the Petrine group sending this letter were Silvanus (v 12), Mark, and an unnamed female (v 13, **she who is . . . likewise chosen;** the Greek term is "co-elect"). The omission of further personal identification implies that these persons were well-known to the addressees in Asia Minor and represented personal bonds between recipients and senders. It is therefore likely that the Silvanus and Mark named here were the same figures of note who appear in Acts and Paul's letters. Both were members of the brotherhood in Jerusalem and both had early personal contacts with Peter. In John Mark's house, Peter had found refuge in his flight from Herod Agrippa (Acts 12:1-17). Later in Jerusalem, Silvanus, (or Silas as he is called by his Aramaic name in Acts), a prophet and one of the "leading men among the brethren" there (Acts 15:22, 27, 32), along with Peter (Acts 15:7-11), played a prominent role at the Apostolic council when he delivered the decision concerning the universal mission to the Gentiles from Jerusalem to Antioch (Acts 15:22-34). Mark and Silvanus also had each accompanied Paul on different phases of his mission through Asia Minor. Mark's early association with Paul terminated after the so-called first missionary journey, according to Acts (13:4-13; 15:36-39), though it is possible that he may have rejoined Paul later (see Col. 4:10; Philemon 24; 2 Tim. 4:11). Silvanus/Silas thereafter accompanied Paul across Asia Minor on the so-called second missionary journey which took them as far as Greece (Acts 15:40—18:22; 2 Cor. 1:19; 1 Thess. 1:1; 2 Thess. 1:1). Eventually, as 1 Peter 5:12-13 suggests, following their association with Paul, both men joined the apostle Peter in forming a Christian group at Rome.

These movements of the apostolic co-workers would account for their being known to the addressees of 1 Peter. Some scholars, furthermore, have seen in Silvanus' association with both Peter and Paul an explanation of certain similarities between 1 Peter on the one hand and the Pauline letters on the other. If all this evidence does refer to the same two persons, what it does suggest in general is that all three persons expressly named in 1 Peter represented important figures through whom the Palestinian Christian tradition of Jesus' words and deeds and the kerygma of his death and resurrection was transmitted from East to West. Thus they represented the universal spread of the universalist gospel proclaimed in 1 Peter from the land of its origin to the capital of the Roman Empire. (For more extensive discussion see John H. Elliott, *A Home for the Homeless*, 1981, in the bibliography.)

The fraternal and familial characterizations of Silvanus as **faithful brother** and of Mark as **my son** (i.e. Peter's spiritual child and disciple) represent a final emphasis on the household nature of the worldwide Christian community. In this context **she who is** (co-elect) **at Babylon** (v 13) most likely implies reference to a Christian sister in the faith. Co-elect, **(likewise chosen)** like co-heirs **(joint heirs** 3:7) and co-elder **(fellow elder** 5:1)—all of which occur only here in the New Testament—

express the common bond that unites the senders and recipients. Likewise, as the recipients are visiting strangers in the Dispersion in Asia Minor (1:1), so the senders reside as aliens in the "Babylon" of Rome.

Babylon was the capital of the mighty empire which six centuries earlier had conquered the nation of Judah and which had become the place of exile of God's people. In prophecy and apocalyptic, Babylon came to represent the anti-godly forces of tyranny, greed, and idolatry (e.g. Isa. 13; 43:14; Jer. 50:29; 51:1-58; the Book of Daniel). After the Roman conquest of Palestine (A.D. 70) the Roman empire and its capital, Rome, was regarded by Jews (4 Ezra 3:1-2; 2 Baruch 11:1; Sibylline Oracles 5:143, 159) and Christians (Rev. 14:8; 16:19; 17:5; 18) as a new Babylon, another idolatrous world power which, like ancient Babylon, could easily absorb and contaminate God's people. In Rome as in Asia Minor the elect were mindful of the pressures for conformity and assimilation and of the need for maintaining a holy and exclusive way of life.

The **kiss of love** (v 14) or "holy kiss" (Rom. 16:16; 1 Cor. 16:20; 2 Cor. 13:12) was a physical embrace used in the natural family and adopted by the Christian family of God as a concrete expression of affection and unity. In the concluding benediction, **in Christ** (as in 3:16, 5:10) indicates the quintessential basis and scope of that unity; and **peace** (see 1:2; 3:11), the divine gift by which it sustained.

The language of the conclusion is similar to that of the salutation (1:1-2). Compare elect/co-elect; Dispersion/Babylon; the familial imagery of Father, brother, (sister), son; grace and peace. This similarity creates an inclusive framework for the entire letter and gives it a formal unity. Even more important, however, is the focus which this framework gives to the letter's message. Although estranged from society, the elect believers in Asia Minor and Rome form one brotherhood or household of God which is united in Christ, called to holy obedience, and sustained by God's grace and peace.

In its own time this vigorous letter of consolation and exhortation gave eloquent witness to the manner in which early Christians confronted the social and religious discrimination of their age with its demand for conformity to popular values, hopeless worldviews, and oppressive institutions. In the confidence of who you are by God's mercy, and how you are to live as God's holy family in a hostile society, the letter affirms, you can overcome evil with good and lead all creatures to the praise of their Creator. In Christian history this letter has found a permanent place in the church's life of liturgy, song, confession, and prayer. For the faithful of all ages its message concerning the distinctive character of Christian community and its divine vocation in society remains a perennial source of inspiration and challenge.

II PETER

John H. Elliott

INTRODUCTION

In contrast to the early and wide reception 1 Peter enjoyed in the ancient church, 2 Peter met with relatively strong resistence. Together with 1 Peter and a large body of non-canonical Petrine literature (including the Apocalypse of Peter, the Gospel of Peter, the Preaching of Peter, the Acts of Peter, and the Pseudo-Clementine writings), 2 Peter illustrates the prominence attributed to the apostle Peter in orthodox and heterodox circles of the early church. Despite its Petrine pedigree, however, no New Testament writing was so poorly attested among the Church Fathers or received into the canon with greater hesitation than was 2 Peter. Down to the present day its canonical status and theological significance seems to have remained more a theory than a fact. Apart from its use in the modern controversies regarding biblical inspiration and authority (esp. 1:20-21), the letter has received relatively short shrift in Christian exegesis, theology and worship.

Luther saw in 2 Peter a refutation of twin errors concerning the doctrine of faith which were rampant in his own day; namely, "the error which ascribes to works the power, which faith alone has, to render a person pious and acceptable to God and, on the other hand, the mistaken notion that faith can exist without good works" (*Luther's Works,* vol. 30, p. 149). For the majority of more recent interpreters, 2 Peter is among the least significant of the New Testament compositions. It has been thought to breathe a different and inferior air than that of the epistles of Paul and even of 1 Peter. Faith, as in

Jude and the Pastorals, has here been objectified and fixed,
the gospel is never explicitly mentioned, its Christology is
minimal, and the letter in general appears to promote a nostal-
gia for the past rather than a confidence in the Spirit's working in the present. In brief, it is regularly regarded, especially
by many Lutheran exegetes, as an unhappy example of the loss
of an authentic evangelical spirit in the church as it moved
into the second century and became preoccupied with internal
heresies and the need for institutional consolidation. On this
view, 2 Peter is more interesting for historical than theological
reasons since it indicates the gradual route taken toward the
formation of a unified Catholic church rather than demon-
strating any attempt at creative theology.

However this current verdict of scholars is to be judged, it
cannot be denied that in practice 2 Peter has been relegated to
the periphery of the church's canon. It seems to have had
little influence on Christian prayer or hymnody, although
echoes of its words may be heard in such hymns as "How Good
Lord to Be Here" and "O God Our Help in Ages Past." In the
revised Lectionary it is appointed for liturgical reading only
twice: on the Festival of the Transfiguration (1:16-19) and on
the Second Sunday in Advent (3:8-14). Nevertheless, like its
compatriot, Jude, this canonical witness to the attempt of the
early church to remain true to its theological heritage amid a
fragmented and skeptical culture deserves careful attention.
For when, as Luther put it, the "Epicureans" of any age scoff
at the rule of God, the certainty of afterlife and judgment, and
the implications of Christ's coming for moral Christian living
in the present, then the message of 2 Peter takes on renewed
urgency and vitality.

1. Literary Type and Pseudonymity of 2 Peter

2 Peter is a document beset with anomalies. Its external
form appears to be that of a letter (1:1-2), but internally it

assumes the character of a farewell discourse or a final testament (1:12-15). It appears to be a testament of the apostle Peter (1:1) composed as a reminder for use in the *future* (1:12-15; 3:1-2); but its message refers to a *present* problem (note the present tense verbs in 2:10b-22; 3:5, 11-18) troubling the church long after Peter's death (c. 65-67). It appears to repeat the content of an earlier letter by the same author (3:2); in actuality, however, the letter it most fully reproduces is the one by Jude. It was composed in a style more influenced by the Greek culture of the second century than any other document in the New Testament. Yet its major aim is a recollection of ancient Jewish-Christian views concerning the end of the world. Its authorship by, or association with, Peter should have secured its early reception into the canon; yet its canonical status was more disputed than that of any other New Testament writing.

2 Peter was composed as a farewell address or testament of the apostle Peter put into a form resembling a letter. Although it begins with a salutation (1:1-2), it lacks a specific address and any indications of a personal relation between sender and recipients. It concludes, as does Jude, not with personal greetings but with a brief benediction (3:18). Its formal character is determined primarily by 1:12-15 which declares this composition to be a record of the last words of Peter prior to his death and intended as a reminder and warning of things to come.

2 Peter thus resembles other farewell addresses or final testaments found in the New Testament (Mark 13 par.; John 13–17; Acts 20:17-35; 2 Tim.) as well as in the Old Testament (Gen. 47:29–49:32; Deut. 1–3; 28–31; Josh. 23–24; 1 Sam. 12) and especially in the Pseudepigrapha of the Intertestamental period (e.g. the Testaments of Abraham, Moses, Job, the Twelve Patriarchs). Much of this latter literature was pseudonymous (from the Greek "falsely named," i.e. attributed to persons other than the real authors). It was common for

Greek, Latin, and Jewish authors to compose writings dealing with current affairs as prophecies and predictions and to attribute them to ancient venerable figures of the distant past (e.g. the Wisdom and Psalms of Solomon, the Books of Enoch, the Book of Daniel, the Sibylline Oracles, the Apocalypses of Abraham, Baruch, Esdras and Sedrach). The early Christians also used this form of pseudonymous composition (e.g. Eph., the Pastorals, James, Jude, 1 and 2 Peter, 2 Clement; Teaching of the Twelve Apostles and many Christian apocryphal writings).

Motives for this kind of composition varied. Association of particular ancient authors or figures with certain types of writing accounts for some instances of pseudonymity (e.g. attribution of epic poetry to Homer and Vergil; speeches to Demosthenes; psalms to David; wisdom literature to Solomon; letters to Seneca and Paul). Disciples of great philosophic and religious leaders attributed their later writings to the inspiration and teaching of their masters (e.g. members of the Academy attributed many of their writings to Plato). In the New Testament, disciples of Paul, Peter, John, James, and Jude also preserved, expanded and transmitted material which was attributed to their original teachers. The type of literature known as *testament* linked events of the present with the anticipations of great figures from the past, and thereby secured for its teaching the authority antiquity confers. This appears to have been the chief motive for attributing 2 Peter to the apostle Peter. For here the apostle teaches by way of reminder (1:12-15; 3:1-2) and leaves behind a testament by which the readers, after his death, **may be able at any time to recall these things** (1:15).

In actuality, the author or authors of this document speak of **your apostles** (3:2, as in Jude 17) as of a group separate from both the composer(s) and recipients of 2 Peter. Moreover, in the shift from future to present tense verbs (cp. 2:1-10a/10b-22; 3:2-4/5-18), prediction is abandoned altogether and the real author speaks to his present situation. 2 Peter is thus a literary fiction in regard to both its epistolary and testamental form and its authorship. Other features to be discussed below corroborate its pseudonymous character. Who actually composed 2 Peter cannot be determined. Ascription of the writing to the apostle Peter rather than, say, to Jude or some other Christian notable at least suggests that 2 Peter, like 1 Peter, originated in some circle of Petrine disciples.

Literary conventions today vary greatly from those of the past. It would therefore be a fundamental mistake to confuse ancient pseudonymous writings such as 2 Peter with forgeries produced from dishonest intention. Pseudonymous writing was a common literary device of the day employed by Jews and Christians alike to link securely the present teaching of synagogue and church to the persons with whom such tradition was honestly and fervently believed to have originated.

2. Literary Composition and Sources

Two further anomalies of 2 Peter involve its chief source and the sophisticated formulation of its "old fashioned" message. **This is now the second letter that I have written to you** (3:1) seems to be an implied reference to the letter known as 1 Peter. However, apart from a common emphasis on the coming of Jesus Christ and the day of judgment and other minor similarities, the stylistic and theological differences far outnumber the similarities between these two writings. 1 Peter has a specific address, confronts the issue of the Christian brotherhood's relation to external society, frequently cites the Old Testament explicitly, and draws on a wide range of Christian tradition which relates it to many other compositions of the New Testament. 2 Peter, by contrast, is vague as to its destination (1:1), confronts a problem of internal dissension (2:1-3), never explicitly quotes from the Old Testament, has no developed Christology or ecclesiology and is

close in content only to the Pastorals and the Letter of Jude
with which it has a unique relationship.

The continuation of 3:1 is virtually identical with Jude 17–
18. In fact the similarity between 2 Peter and Jude is so close
that direct literary dependence is certain. While some scholars, including Luther, believed Jude to have been an excerpt
of 2 Peter, it is now generally agreed that 2 Peter is a later
expansion of Jude. Of the 25 verses of Jude, no less than 19,
in whole or in part, reappear in 2 Peter. 2 Peter 2:3-18 reproduces Jude 4-16 in the same general sequence and with similar or identical wording, some of it unique to these two writings within the New Testament. As 2 Peter 3:2-3 corresponds
to Jude 17-18, so 3:14 and 18 parallel and modify Jude 24-25
and 1:1-2 echo the words of Jude 1-2. Both are incomplete letters ending with benedictions and both denounce ungodly
Christians who have introduced dissent and division into the
Christian community.

On the other hand, 2 Peter is not an exact reproduction but
rather an adaptation and expansion of Jude. The material incorporated from Jude in 2 Peter 2 is set within a larger framework of thought provided by chapters 1 and 3. In addition to
the moral denunciations contained in Jude, 2 Peter describes
and disputes the false teaching of the heretics as well as their
deviant behavior. This use of Jude, together with the alterations and additions made in 2 Peter, provide useful clues to the
situation and strategy of 2 Peter as well as to its date of composition.

Typical of 2 Peter, and another of its many anomalies, is its
use of sophisticated language to promote "old-time religion."
Fifty-six of its 1103 words are unique in the New Testament;
32 of them are foreign to the Greek Old Testament as well. In
contrast to both 1 Peter and Jude, 2 Peter displays a preten-
tious Asiatic style of composition marked by redundancy and
inflated rhetoric. Much of its content also smacks of strong
Greek influence:

- the types of virtues listed in 1:5-7;
- the term for "eyewitness" (1:16) used by the Eleusinian mystery cult in their worship of Demeter and Persephone (cf. also similar terms in 1:9; 2:4);
- reference to death as a putting off of the bodily tent (1:13-14);
- reference to popular myths regarding the gods (1:16);
- allusion to hell or the place of the dead as Tartarus (2:4);
- the depiction of God and/or Jesus Christ as Savior (1:1, 11; 2:20; 3:2, 18);
- the identification of knowledge as a means of access to God (1:2, 3, 6, 8, 12; 2:20, 21; 3:3, 17, 18) and of salvation and life as godliness (1:3), escape from the world and participation in divine being (1:4).

This author is conversant with

1) the public celebration of saviors and benefactors,
2) the current philosophies, especially that of the pleasure-oriented Epicureans,
3) the importance attributed to knowledge as a means to perfection, enlightenment, happiness or union with divinity,
4) the language of the mystery religions and especially the teachings and practice of half-baked rationalists and skeptics who dispute divine providence, life after death, and post-mortem retribution.

With this new religious vocabulary, the author appeals to the ancient testimonies of God's creative and judging activity (2:1-22; 3:1-10), his power to destroy, make alive (1:3-11), and grant entrance into the eternal kingdom (1:11), an earlier image for life with God which, since the kingdom proclamation of Jesus, had rarely been used in the Christian mission to the Gentiles.

Anomalous as all these features of 2 Peter may be, they nevertheless are useful for situating the document and assessing its message. As the Greek character and content of 2 Peter illuminate its historical and cultural situation, so its source and teaching shed light on its aim and strategy.

The Greek text and syntax of 2 Peter is often unclear. On the whole, however, an integrated line of thought is discernible. Following a greeting (1:1-2) and a preamble (1:3-11) comes a reminder of the apostolic and prophetic tradition here used to denounce the false teachers (1:12—3:13). The letter concludes with an exhortation (3:14-18) pertaining to the gifts and responsibilities of the faithful. Within these major sections the units 1:12-15, 16-21; 2:1-22; 3:1-7, 8-13 are marked off by their content as well as by the introductory address, **beloved** (3:1, 8, 14). Linkwords (e.g. **knowledge**, 1:2, 3, 8; **borne**, 1:17, 18; **prophecy**, 1:19-21; 2:1; **ignore**, 3:5, 8; **forbearance**, 3:9, 15 etc.) as well as the frequent use of demonstratives (**these things,** 1:8, 9, 10, 12; 2:20; 3:11, 14) relate and join units of thought and, together with a consistent vocabulary and style, provide literary integrity to the letter as a whole.

3. Situation and Strategy

The situation confronted in 2 Peter is summarized briefly in 2:1-3. Among the recipients will come (i.e. already have come, 2:10b-22; 3:5-7, 16-17) **false teachers,** who, like the false prophets of old and especially greedy Balaam (2:15-16), introduce on the sly destructive and divisive opinions and engage in licentious and greedy conduct. This combination of false words and exploitative behavior undermines the stability and solidarity of the Christian community. In 2:4—3:13 the disruptive impact of these apostates (2:20-22) on the community is detailed, especially their denying **the Master who bought them** (2:1). Their slogan was "freedom for all" (2:19), yet they sought not the communal good but enticed unstable converts and exploited other members as they pursued their own greedy purposes 2:3, 14). Claiming a superior knowledge (which 2 Peter forcefully disputes in 2:12, 16, 18, 20-21; 3:5-7, 16), and spewing forth boasts and reviling, they distorted the Christian tradition through private interpretation in order to legitimate their erroneous teaching and actions. This teaching involved not only a notion of freedom *for* the flesh (rather than *from* the flesh, 2:19-21) but also freedom from the "myth" of God's involvement in human affairs and his judging of human actions at the coming of the day of the Lord (3:1-13). Using the theme of liberty as a pretext for self-indulgence, these false teachers not only endangered the inner cohesion of the Christian community but also caused the **way of truth** to be reviled by outsiders (2:2).

The situation described in 2 Peter has often suggested to scholars the circumstances of the second century when the emergence of Christian Gnostic groups threatened the unity of faith and the solidarity of the Christian movement. Similarities between the false teachers of 2 Peter and such Gnostics (as described by Irenaeus in *Against Heresies,* c. A.D. 185) are indeed numerous. In varying ways these Gnostics also promoted a moral freedom and a religious teaching quite different from that of orthodox Christian circles and based it upon a source of knowledge *(gnosis* in Greek, whence the term "Gnostic") which was independent of the prophetic and apostolic tradition. The repeated stress in 2 Peter on an authentic knowledge as well as the emphasis on a correct understanding of the apostolic and prophetic tradition, suggests an interest in refuting persons making claims to special knowledge.

Interest in wisdom and knowledge as a means to enlightenment, perfection or salvation, however, was by no means restricted to these heretical Christian groups of the second century and later. Secular groups such as the school of Epicurus (341-270 B.C.) propounded views and practices with which the false teachers of 2 Peter seem to have had much in common. To the outsider as well as to many a Christian convert, Epicureanism and Christianity appeared to have many similar themes including their repudiation of popular religion, their sectarian exclusiveness, and the close bond of friendship that united their adherents. In the popular mind the two groups were closely associated and commonly subjected to the same condemnation. Much of what 2 Peter describes as **destructive heresies** (2:1) seems to have been the result of the influence of Epicurean thought on Christian doctrine.

The situation called for rapid remedy. The forces that divided the community had to be exposed and expunged, and the faithful had to be confirmed in the way of truth and righteousness. The strategy of the letter therefore involved the combination of a rebuke of the apostates with a reaffirmation of the faithful. Here, as in Jude, the false teachers are compared with condemned sinners of old (ch. 2) and are contrasted to the faithful (chs. 1 and 3). Beyond Jude, however, 2 Peter also refutes the *content* of their teaching. What the false teachers claim for themselves, namely knowledge and freedom from all conventional norms, 2 Peter denies (ch. 2). What they ignore, namely God's action in past, present, and future, 2 Peter reaffirms (1:16-19; 3:1-13). The apostolic and prophetic witness, which they distort with individualist interpretation (1:20-21; 3:1-13, 15-16), 2 Peter clarifies anew. In contrast to the ignorant apostates, the addressees are reminded of what they already have by God's power (1:3-11) and what they already know (1:12). Their continued growth in these divine gifts and their recollection of the apostolic and prophetic witness is the means by which they might detect and refute error in their midst and thereby defend themselves against those who would mislead them.

Since the error under attack had more to do with morality than with doctrines about Christ or the church, 2 Peter does not base its instruction on the teaching of Christ's death and resurrection (as do Paul and 1 Peter) but on the implications of God's rule over the world. In order to refute those who tried to use the teaching of Paul as a basis for their own teachings and morality (3:15-16), and to assure the readers of the apostolic basis of his own words, the author of 2 Peter appealed to the weighty eyewitness tradition of the apostle Peter (1:16-18) and presented his letter as the apostle's last will and testament (1:1, 12-15; 3:1).

2 Peter might be considered radical in a double sense. On the one hand, it represents a radical adaptation of the Christian gospel to the language and culture of Greco-Roman secular society. On the other hand, to head off a dangerous deterioration of Christian morality and a loss of confidence in God's sustaining power, it reminds the readers of their roots *(radix* in Latin, whence "radical"), their ancient traditions and their corresponding responsibilities.

4. Origin, Destination, and Date

2 Peter contains no explicit information regarding the identity or location of its intended recipients or its place of origin. Its vocabulary could have been influenced by any cosmopolitan center of the Mediterranean world such as Antioch in Syria, Alexandria in Egypt, Ephesus in Asia Minor, or Rome. The strongest evidence, however, relates 2 Peter to the thought world and culture of Asia Minor. Here the predominantly Gentile Christian addressees of the letter would have the same cultural and religious background as the author. Asia Minor as the place of composition and destination of the letter is further supported by the existence of Epicurean groups, the circulation of Pauline letters, and by the fact that Christians there had received the letter of 1 Peter to which 2 Peter 3:1 most likely refers. Egypt, however, also remains a possibility as its place of destination, particularly since the existence of 2 Peter is first attested there in the *Apocalypse of Peter* (c. A.D. 135), and since Origen (217-251), a resident of Alexandria, was the first author of the patristic period to cite it explicitly (Eusebius, *Ecclesiastical History*, 6.25).

2 Peter's use of Jude (written c. 70-100), its allusion to

1 Peter (written c. 75-92), and the probable use of 2 Peter in the Apocalypse of Peter (c. 135) set the lower and higher limits of its date of composition. The internal Christian divisions it describes, the delay of the parousia it attempts to explain, its advanced Hellenistic spirit, its affinities primarily with the late Pastorals, its reference to the apostolic teaching of a past generation, its knowledge of a collection of Pauline letters and their status as scripture, and its relatively late attestation, all indicate that 2 Peter is with great likelihood the latest composition of the New Testament, written sometime in the first quarter of the second century.

By this time the apostle Peter had long since died. The letter, therefore, must have been written by Christians of Asia Minor who represented the Petrine legacy. Together with 1 Peter, this letter attests the increasing importance attributed to Peter, the apostle and eyewitness of the Lord, as guarantor of the apostolic faith in the church's continuing struggle to preserve and articulate its "one, holy, catholic and apostolic" identity.

OUTLINE OF 2 PETER

1:1-2 *Symeon Peter, slave and apostle of Jesus Christ, to our equals in the faith: Greeting!*

■ *1:3-11* *All things pertaining to life and godliness are ours. Confirm your divine calling through godly conduct.*

1:3-4 *We who have received God's gifts and promises have escaped the world's corruption.*

1:5-11 *You, therefore, make every effort to supplement faith with faithful behavior, thereby confirming your divine call.*

■ *1:12—3:13* *Remember the apostolic and prophetic teaching, which confirms you in the way of truth and refutes those who live and teach the way of error.*

1:12-15 *I remind you of these things so that later you may recall them.*

131

1:16-21   *The basis of our knowledge of the power and
          parousia of our Lord Jesus Christ is the apostolic
          and prophetic witness to God's word and work-
          ing.*

2:1-22   *The divisive false teachers among you stand con-
          demned.*

3:1-13   *I remind you again: contrary to the skepticism of
          the scoffers, the coming of the Lord is certain.*

■ 3:14-18 *Wait for the Lord in grace and knowl-
          edge, peace and holiness.*

COMMENTARY

1:1-2 *Symeon Peter, slave and apostle of Jesus Christ, to our equals in the faith: Greeting!*

The testament of the apostle Peter has been put in the form of a letter by his disciples and has been sent to troubled Christians as a reminder of the truth, knowledge, and virtue in which they are to grow. Like Jude, however, and in contrast to 1 Peter, this composition does not locate its addressees or indicate any personal contact between recipients and sender(s). It thus belongs to the most general of the Catholic Epistles (which include James, 1–2 Peter, 1–2–3 John and Jude).

1a—The addition of "Symeon," the Semitic form of the apostle's name (used elsewhere only in Acts 15:14), to **Peter,** ("Rock") by which Simon Bar-Jona (Matt. 16:17; John 1:42) generally came to be known, lends verisimilitude to the Petrine stamp of the letter. This writing, it affirms, contains the testimony of that Palestinian Symeon Peter who was an original eyewitness of the historical Jesus (see 1:16-18. On Peter in general see the commentary on 1 Peter 1:1; on "servant/slave" see the commentary on Jude 1). The idea of slave as one who is bought and owned expresses the apostle's relation to Jesus Christ, the Master who bought him (see 2:1).

1b—The language here, as throughout the rest of 2 Peter,

has been conditioned by the Hellenistic environment of the author. Familiar terms of the Christian tradition are used and infused with different Hellenistic meanings. God and Jesus Christ are portrayed as the greatest of the world's Saviors and Benefactors (also 1:11; 2:20; 3:2, 18) whose gifts to the believers (vv 3-4) entail responsibilities on the part of the recipients (vv 5-7). Thus **faith** in v 1b has the sense not of response to Jesus as Christ and Lord or obedient trust in God (as e.g., in Paul and 1 Peter) but faith is commitment to responsibility. **Righteousness,** likewise, refers not to God's paradoxical pardon of the guilty or to his covenantal fidelity but to the equity and fairness with which these great benefactions and responsibilities have been distributed equally to the addressees as well as to the apostles (**a faith of equal standing with ours,** i.e. the apostles). Through the fairness of their great Patron and Bene-factor, the addressees, it is said, "enjoy equal privilege" (NEB) with the apostles of old. (On the motif of Benefactors and Re-cipients in 2 Peter and its cultural background, see the studies of F. W. Danker in the Bibliography. On **Savior,** see the com-mentary on Jude 3–4; compare 2 Peter's usage to Jude where "Savior" applies to God only. In 1 Peter the term is never used.)

2—The greeting resembles 1 Peter 1:2 (cf. **be multiplied** also in Jude 2). However, the addition **in the** *knowledge* **of God and of Jesus our Lord** introduces one of the special accents of 2 Peter. The "full knowledge" which God confers on the be-lievers through that which the apostles and prophets have made known is the **knowledge** in which the recipients are to grow so that they can effectively resist the false teaching and enticements of the apostates. Thus knowledge and its con-trast to ignorance is a theme which pervades the letter from start to finish.

■ *1:3-11   All things pertaining to life and godliness are ours. Confirm your divine calling through godly conduct.*

A preamble, not clearly separated from vv 1b-2, describes the lavish gifts and promises the believers have received from their divine Savior and Benefactor (vv 3-4) and the reciprocal moral responsibilities these gifts entail (vv 5-7). Then the preamble contrasts those who act responsibly with those who do not (vv 8-9), and concludes with an emphasis on the glorious prospect of eternal life for those who remain faithful (vv 10-11). This message introduces the qualities that distinguish true believers from false teachers (2:1ff.) and compares the eternal kingdom that awaits the former with the certain condemnation already earned by the latter.

1:3-4 *We who have received God's gifts and promises have escaped the world's corruption.*

Here, as elsewhere in the letter (1:10; 2:4, 6, 13, 20, 21; 3:5-6, 10, 11) the text and/or syntax is uncertain. The RSV translation smoothes over the fact that vv 3-4 lack a main verb and do not form a complete sentence. Nevertheless, since the greeting of v 2 provides a natural termination for vv 1-2, vv 3-11 are best taken as a related yet separate unit. The unusual phrases **divine power** and **divine nature,** which occur nowhere else in the New Testament, frame vv 3-4. As a parallel to **call** and **election** and **kingdom** (vv 10-11), these verses describe in more Hellenistic fashion the means and goal of Christian existence. It is also unclear whether **his** and **he** in these verses refers to God or to Jesus Christ (vv 1, 2). In contrast to the earlier church (e.g. 1 Cor. 8:6; 1 Peter 1:3; 4:11 etc.), the author has not preserved a clear distinction between the identity and action of God, on the one hand, and Jesus Christ on the other. As in the later New Testament writings (e.g. John 20:28; Titus 2:13) and extra-canonical writings (e.g. Ignatius, *Ephesians* inscr. and 1:1), Jesus Christ is seen to share in the attributes and actions of God. In the environment of 2 Peter, to regard the exalted Lord as **divine** would be to attribute to him the same type of divinity (i.e. especially favored by the gods/God) for which emperors, public benefactors, powerful saviors and virtuous philosophers were celebrated.

Here in 2 Peter the readers are assured that they are the recipients of the gifts of the Supreme Savior and Benefactor who has given them **all things that pertain to life and godliness.** Baptism and conversion have liberated believers from domination by the passions of the world (v 4; see 2:19-20) and have subjected them to the rule of the **Lord and Savior Jesus Christ** (1:2, 8, 11, 14, 16; 3:2, 18). As **godliness** is the opposite of moral corruption, so **life** is the contrast to death and corruptibility. Implicit here is perhaps a repudiation of the Epicurean notion, held by some of the opponents, that all matter, being composed of atoms which eventually disintegrate, tends inexorably toward corruption and decay. Believers who are united with the life-giving One, however, partake of his divine and incorruptible nature. This concept of union with God, while typical of Greek thought, is unique in the New Testament. Compare, e.g. 1 Peter 4:13 and 5:1 where Christians are said to share not the **divine nature** but the sufferings of Christ and the glories of his resurrection. The adoption of the idea of sharing in the divine nature is a graphic illustration of how, in the history of Christian controversy, the rejection of new versions of error has often led to the use of new and "relevant" terminology.

These gifts and promises, through which escape from the world's corruption has been made possible, are ours **through the knowledge of him who called us** (perhaps an echo of 1 Peter 2:9, 21; 3:9; 5:10). **Promises** alludes to one of the chief issues under dispute among the addressees. It is the promises of the Lord's coming (1:16; 3:3-4) and the divine judgment of human action it involves (3:5-7) which the scoffers ridicule. Claiming to live in an unchanging present devoid of God's presence (3:3-7), they are led only by their own self-serving desires and entice others to follow suit (ch 2). The addressees, therefore, are advised that these promises will indeed be realized (3:8-13). Hence they must make every effort not to lose or squander what they have been given.

To (or "by") **his own glory and excellence** identifies the divine virtues with reference to which the believers are also to be "virtuous" (v 5). Likewise, the **knowledge** and **godliness** given by God is the same knowledge and godliness in which the recipients are to grow (vv 5, 6, 7; 3:11, 18). Verses 3-4 thus describe the divine initiative that establishes the basis for the imperatives that follow (vv 5-11).

1:5-11 You, therefore, make every effort to supplement faith with faithful behavior, thereby confirming your divine call.

The picturesque verb *epichoregein* rendered **supplement** in v 5 and **will be provided** in v 11 frames this second unit. This verb originally pertained to the world of Greek drama where a wealthy individual called a *choregos* paid the expenses of the chorus and helped produce the plays. Later it was used of rich benefactors whose generosity supplied a city's needs. Here it portrays the cooperation between God the "producer of the Christian drama," as it were, and those who are the recipients and emulators of his generosity. The divine gifts and promises call for corresponding action on the part of their beneficiaries.

5-7—A climactic chain of eight virtues (a numerical symbol of perfection; cf. Noah's family, 2:5) enumerates the actions by which the addressees are to manifest their escape from the world's corruption and their union with God (vv 3-4). Except for **faith** and **love** with which the list begins and ends, these virtues are more typical of qualities prized in the Greco-Roman world than in the literature of the early Christians. (For New Testament lists of virtues see 2 Cor. 6:6; Gal. 5:22-23; Eph. 4:2-3, 32; 5:9; Phil. 4:8; Col. 3:12; 1 Tim. 4:12; 6:11; 2 Tim.

2:22; 3:10; 1 Peter 3:8). The virtues enumerated here, however, owe their presence not simply to cultural influence in general but to the situation confronted by 2 Peter in particular. These virtues are precisely the features by which the true believers are to distinguish themselves from the false teachers in their midst.

Whereas the false teachers have again become enslaved in the world (2:19-22), the true believers are to make their **escape** (v 4) a constant reality. **For this very reason** their character and conduct must reflect the divine nature in which they share. The commitment to responsibility, **faith,** which they have obtained (v 1) must be supplemented by moral excellence *(aretē,* translated **excellence** in v 3 and **virtue** in v 5) which corresponds to the noble largesse of God and contrasts to the greed of false prophets (2:3, 14-15). In similar contrasting fashion, the believers are to cultivate

- **knowledge** which sets them apart from the ignorant apostates;
- **self-control** in contrast to the latter's unbridled licentiousness (2:2, 18; 3:3; cf. 2:7);
- **steadfastness** (and stability, 1:10, 12; 3:17) over against the defection of the false teachers (2:19-22) and the instability of their prey (2:2, 18);
- **godliness** ("piety") which resists the latter's ungodliness (3:7; cf. 2:5, 6); and
- **brotherly affection** and **love** which unites the believers against those who would tear the community apart (2:1).

8-9—The contrast implicit in the preceding verses is now made explicit. If the recipients abound in the virtues just outlined, then these virtues will keep them from being useless and fruitless in respect to the knowledge of the Lord (vv 3, 5). Verse 9, on the other hand, anticipates the blind condition of the apostates. Whoever lacks these qualities is **blind** to the enlightenment Christian baptism brings (cf. Heb. 6:4; 10:32). Such people have forgotten their baptismal cleansing from sin (see Acts 22:16; 1 Cor. 6:11; 1 Peter 1:22), as have the apostates (2:19-22). While the defectors forget and ignore (3:5-7), the addressees are to remember (1:12, 13, 15; 3:1-2) and "not ignore" (3:8-10).

10-11—The final verses of the preamble tie the unit together and stress again the strenuous effort the addressees must make to achieve the goal of their calling. **Be the more zealous** parallels in Greek the expression **make every effort** in v 5; **provided** repeats in Greek the verb rendered **supplement** in v 5; **call and election** echo **called** in v 3; and **entrance into the eternal kingdom** restates in more familiar terms the goal of participation in the **divine nature** (v 4).

In the face of divisive threats to their personal and communal stability, the readers are enjoined to **confirm,** i.e. "make sure and certain," cf. 1:19) their divine **call and election** (see Matt. 22:14; Rom. 8:28-30; 1 Cor. 1:26-27; 1 Peter 2:9; Rev. 17:14) so that they might **never fall** (cf. Jude 24) in the sense of being **carried away with the error of lawless men and losing stability** (3:17). God's generous gifts and promises make their supplemental actions (vv 5-7) possible and provide for them an **entrance into the eternal kingdom.** In contrast to the unfaithful who in their moral corruption are enslaved in a perishing world (2:3, 4-10, 19; 3:5-7, 10-12), those who confirm their calling with steadfast fidelity will enjoy life in a kingdom that endures forever.

■ *1:12—3:13   Remember the apostolic and prophetic teaching, which confirms you in the way of truth and refutes those who live and teach the way of error.*

This central section of 2 Peter is a combination of reminder, reproach, and refutation. In order to confirm the addressees in

the **truth** or **way of truth** (2:2) in which they are already established (1:12), the author recalls the apostolic and prophetic
witness which should serve as a permanent basis and norm for
recognizing that truth and for detecting and resisting deviation
from **the way of righteousness** (2:21). The subunits of this
section include

  (A) 1:12-15, a statement of the letter's purpose, which is em-
      phasized at beginning (v 12) and end (v 15) as one of
      reminder;

  (B) 1:16-21, a recollection and caution concerning the apos-
      tolic and prophetic tradition with which the readers are
      already acquainted (vv 16, 20);

  (C) 2:1-22, a denunciation of false teachers which is framed
      at commencement and close with a reference to the way
      of truth/righteousness (2:2, 21); and

  (D) 3:1-13, a second reminder (vv 1-4), refutation and caution
      (vv 5-13) concerning the certainty of the Lord's final
      coming in judgment.

1:12-15   I remind you of these things so that later you may recall them.

The content of the letter is here characterized as Peter's last
will and testament; the author is its preserver and executor.
(See Section 1 of the Introduction.) The **truth** (v 12) to which
Peter's words bear witness is to be a permanent record that
must be later recalled (vv 12, 15; 3:1-2). The authority of this
witness is established by the fact that Peter was among those
to whom the very **voice** or word of God was **borne** (vv 17-18).
This **reminder** (cf. Jude 5) of what the addressees have already
received (1:3-11), of what they **know** (1:12, 16; 3:1-2), should
understand (1:20; 3:3) and **not ignore** (3:8-13) was, according
to vv 13-14, given sometime before the apostle's death. The
idea of the nearness or suddenness (**soon,** v 14) of Peter's **de-**

parture (death) could be related to the Petrine tradition preserved in John 21:18-19 and 1 Peter 5:1, and is perhaps echoed in the later Quo Vadis legend of the late second century (Acts of Peter 35).

As long as I am in this body (lit. "tent") reflects the Greek notion of the physical body as a tent. To put off my tent (RSV: **body**) thus becomes a euhemism for "to die" (see 2 Cor. 5:1-5). It is likely, however, that this figurative language for death, including the term *exodus* (RSV: **departure,** v 15), has been influenced by the transfiguration account that follows in vv 16-18 (see *exodus* and "tents" in Luke's transfiguration narrative, Luke 9:28-36). In v 15, **I will see to it,** which renders the same Greek verb used in 1:5 and 10, is a bit weak for the sense implied; namely, "I too, like you, will make an effort" (on behalf of your confirmation). Verse 15 refers to the reminder contained in 2 Peter itself. However, it is general enough to have been understood as a reference to any of the later writings which were also traced to Peter (e.g., Apocalypse of Peter, Gospel of Peter) or even to Mark's gospel which was understood to have derived from Peter.

1:16-21 *The basis of our knowledge of the power and parousia of our Lord Jesus Christ is the apostolic and prophetic witness to God's word and working.*

The main doctrinal theme of the letter is now introduced: the reality of the Lord's **power and coming** (v 16a) and the double basis of its confirmation, namely the combined apostolic (vv 16b-18) and prophetic (vv 19-21) testimony. Since, as becomes clearer in ch. 3, this witness has been disputed (3:2-4) and distorted (3:16), it is imperative that it not only be recalled but clarified at the very outset. The views of the false teachers are implied in the denial of v 16, **we did not follow cleverly devised myths,** and in the corrective statement of v 20, **no**

prophecy of scripture is a matter of one's own interpretation.
In vv 16-18 and 19-21, each of these positions is addressed in
a manner that demonstrates the unity and underlying divine
authority of the apostolic and prophetic word and hence the
certainty of the Lord's coming which they attest.

16-18—At issue within the congregation addressed in 2 Peter
was the reality of the Lord Jesus Christ's power and parousia,
i.e., his exalted status as divine Lord and his final coming in
glory and judgment (see 3:3-7 and the commentary there on
the term *parousia*). Some of the members had begun to scoff
at the idea of the Lord's coming (3:3). Basing their skepticism
on historical experience they argued: **ever since the fathers fell
asleep, all things have continued as they were from the beginning of creation** (3:4). On the basis of such evidence, they could
disparage the apostolic proclamation as nothing more than a
concoction of **cleverly devised myths** (1:16). Such disparage-
ment of popularly held religious ideas as myths (i.e., fabulous
stories about the gods) and appeal to sensate experience, suggests the influence here of Epicurean thought and tactics. The
strategy of 2 Peter is to fight fire with fire—in more ways than
one (see 3:7, 10, 12). The Lord's **power and coming** are indeed
certain because the apostles who made it known were themselves witnesses to his majesty (vv 16-18). **We** personally saw
it and **heard** it confirmed by the divine **voice borne from
heaven, for we were with him on the holy mountain.**

The personal experience to which reference is made is the
transfiguration of Jesus (see Matt. 17:1-8; Mark 9:2-8; Luke
9:28-36; cf. Acts of Peter 20). At this event when the majestic
Father confirmed the majesty of his Son in a prefiguration of
his resurrection and coming in full glory, the apostles Peter,
James, and John were a select group of eyewitnesses who *saw*
Jesus' honor and glory and *heard* **God's voice borne from
heaven** (vv 17, 18). While it was the experience of the risen
rather than of the transfigured Jesus that established the cre-
dentials of the apostles and thus also of Paul (see Rom. 1:1-5;

1 Cor. 15:3-11; Gal. 1:1, 12), the transfiguration experience is cited here because it included not only the *vision* of Jesus' glory but also the *hearing* of God's voice/word. Emphasis of this twofold experience serves a double purpose. On the one hand, it helps to demonstrate the similarity and unity of the apostolic and prophetic witness. On the other, it provides a basis for refuting the charge of propagating **myths.** For a similar emphasis on multiple sense experiences as an authentication of apostolic proclamation see 1 John 1:1-4: "That which we have seen and heard we proclaim also to you."

19-21—To make his case still stronger the author adds to the apostolic experience the witness of sacred scripture (**prophetic word, prophecy of scripture** embracing the entire Old Testament as in Acts 3:24 and 1 Peter 1:10-12). Scriptural prophecy also testifies to the coming of the Lord and through the experience of the apostles that testimony has been **made more sure** and reliable (v 19). The similarity and unity of the apostolic and the prophetic word is expressed in two distinctive ways:

1) The power and coming of the Lord is symbolized by the image of light (**glory,** v 17; **lamp, day, morning star,** v 19);

2) Similar or identical Greek terms are used to depict the divine role in the experience of both apostles and prophets. (**Voice, word, spoke,** vv 17, 19, 21; Gk. *phero* is used four times and is translated **borne** in vv 17, 18, and **came** and **moved** in v 21.)

19—The **prophetic word,** like a **lamp shining in a dark place** (i.e., this present age) announces what the apostles have now confirmed; namely, the certainty of the coming of the Lord. Therefore the recipients are to heed this word until its light is superseded by the appearance of the "light-bearer" and the advent of the full light of day (i.e., the day of the Lord, 3:3, 8, 12). "Light-bearer" is the literal rendition of the Greek *phōsphoros* (RSV: **morning star**). In Judaism, the prophecy of Num. 24:17 ("a star shall come forth out of Jacob") was understood as a reference to the coming Messiah (Testament of Levi 18:3;

Testament of Judah 24:1-5). Christians thought of Jesus as a
bearer of light and accordingly spoke of him as the dawn from
on high (Luke 1:78) and "the bright morning star" (Rev. 22:16).
Rises in your hearts contrasts the enlightened Christian community of the end time to those scoffers for whom the coming
of the Lord will mean not illumination but destruction (3:7).

20-21—This prophetic word, however, as the false teachers
have already shown (3:16), is susceptible to distortion. The
readers therefore must understand that the Holy Spirit from
whom this word originated (v 21) also controls its interpretation (v 20). Engaging in **one's** *own* (private) **interpretation** (in
order to legitimate private divisive opinions, 2:1) implies an
activity running counter to the interpretation of the Christian
community as a whole. The pursuit of **their** *own* **passions** (3:3;
cf. 2:22; 3:16) was a cardinal defect of the false teachers who
thereby resembled **false prophets** (2:1). Like Balaam (2:15)
they manifested the classical features of false prophets who
spoke their *own* words contrary to what God intended (see
e.g. Jer. 23:16; Ezek. 13:3). **Prophecy of scripture,** however,
like the apostolic word, originates not in the will (RSV: **impulse)**
of human beings. Both derive, rather, from the action of God.
As the divine voice was **borne** to the apostles with the transfigured Jesus (vv 17, 18), so **men** who were borne (RSV: **moved)**
by the Holy Spirit spoke from God (v 21). Those who scoff at
these words challenge not only the combined authority of the
apostles and prophets but the very authority of God with whom
their words originate.

Although no direct mention of the opponents was made in
this section, its several points of contact with chapters 2 and 3
leave no doubt that it was the divisive opinions of the false
teachers that were here implicitly addressed. At the same time
the readers are also assured that, contrary opinion notwith-
standing, the apostolic and prophetic word is a reliable witness
to the coming of the Lord because it originates with persons
who directly experienced the word and working of God.

2:1-22 *The divisive false teachers among you stand condemned.*

Having established the authoritative and reliable basis on which his message rests (1:12-21), the author now turns to a vehement denunciation of the false teachers in his audience. The reference to **false prophets . . . among the people** (i.e. ancient Israel) in v 1 provides a contrast to the true nature of prophecy described in 1:19-21. To these false prophets of old are compared **false teachers** who will arise **among you,** the holy people of the end time. This comparison of earlier time and end time was a characteristic feature of Christian apocalyptic thought. Thus like Jude 4-16, the bulk of which is incorporated in this section of 2 Peter, events and persons of the past are used to describe events and persons of the final age.

In addition to the Old Testament examples, much of the content here, like that in Jude, involves stock charges of greed, deception, libertinism, and hedonism which were often leveled against sophists and Epicureans in secular circles and in Jewish circles against sinners and "adulterous idolaters" contaminated by foreign culture. All of this material (vv 4-18) is framed by vv 1-3 and vv 19-22 which specify more precisely the grounds for the attack. The troublemakers are identified as false teachers and apostates who introduce on the sly destructive heresies that endanger the cohesion of the community and its missionary efforts.

Beside these additions which have no parallel in Jude, 2 Peter has altered Jude in other significant ways:

- Verses 4-10a (cp Jude 5-8) omit Jude's reference to the desert generation, arrange the Old Testament examples chronologically, and add references to Noah and Lot.
- In vv 10b-18, the legend of the Michael-Devil dispute (cp Jude 9), the mention of Cain and Korah (cp Jude 11), and the citation of 1 Enoch (cp Jude 14-15), have all been eliminated.

These omissions and rearrangements result in the exclusion of all references to noncanonical writings and alter the thoroughly negative illustrations of Jude by creating a balance between the destruction of the ungodly and the salvation of the righteous.

Finally, these alterations of the material taken over from Jude have also introduced certain unclarities of expression (esp. in vv 10b and 17) which can only be deciphered through a comparison with the original text of Jude.

Once the technicalities of composition have been clarified, the message of this section becomes apparent. Deviant teaching, hinted at in 1:16-21 and refuted explicitly in 3:1-13, is accompanied by deviant conduct, according to 2 Peter 2. History, however, teaches that as God rescues the righteous so he shall surely condemn and destroy such unrighteousness. Verses 1-3 introduce and summarize the activities of the false teachers; vv 4-10a cite lessons from sacred history; and vv 10b-22 denounce the immoral conduct of the apostates which earns them condemnation. Reference to the **way of truth** (v 2) and the **way of righteousness** (v 21) frames the unit as a whole.

1-3—As in earlier times **false prophets** arose in Israel (in opposition to the true prophets who spoke from God, vv 19-21), so there will be **(in the last days,** see 3:3) **false teachers among you** (v 1). The future tense verbs in vv 1-3 convey the semblance of an apostolic prediction regarding the future in line with 1:12-15. From 2:10b onward, however, the shift from future to present tense makes it clear that from the standpoint of the present author these false teachers were no longer a future prospect but a present reality. What the apostle had once anticipated in the meantime had come to pass.

The term **false teachers** *(pseudodidaskaloi)* occurs here for the first and only time in secular as well as biblical Greek. It was apparently coined on the pattern of other derogatory "pseudo-" formations such as false witness, false brethren, false Christs, and false prophets. For Christians the appearance of such deviant teaching and "pseudo" types was a signal of the final age (Matt. 24:11, 23-26; Mark 13:22; 1 John 4:1-3; Rev. 16:13; 19:20; 20:10). Motivating the exposé of 2 Peter was the admonition of the Lord: you will recognize them by their deeds (Matt. 7:15).

The teachers, along with the apostles and prophets, held a position of great influence in the Christian community (see Acts 13:1; Rom. 12:6-8; 1 Cor. 12:28-29; Eph. 4:11). This presented persons who once enjoyed the respect of the believers the opportunity of passing off as the truth **destructive heresies** they had "smuggled in" (cf Jude 4) in order to gain a private following. The term **heresies** (from the Greek *haereseis*) connoted not only deviant opinions themselves but also the groups and sects that held those opinions. In the post-apostolic period, heresy was used as a condemnatory label for any manifestation of doctrine and deportment contrary to Christian orthodoxy.

In the case of 2 Peter, the distortion of the truth involved **denying the Master who bought them** (i.e. Christ's power and authority over them, 1:16 and 2:10a) coupled with **licentiousness** (v 2, also vv 7, 18; see Jude 4 and the comment there) and division-mongering (**many will follow,** v 2; cf v 18). This not only undermined the solidarity and stability of the community; it also brought Christianity (**the way of truth**) into disrepute among the nonbelievers and thereby impeded the effective recruitment of new members.

The heresies of the false teachers are therefore branded as heresies of destruction which will bring upon their propagators a **destruction** which will be as **swift** and certain as was the destruction of the world in the flood (see 3:6 and 2:5). The fact that **from of old** (v 3) God has not been inactive (**idle** or **asleep;** see Pss. 44:23; 121:4 for this image) as the scoffers suppose (3:3-4) but has consistently condemned such ungodly people (2:6) is then illustrated in the examples that follow (vv 4-10a).

4-10a—In a revision and expansion of material from Jude 5-8, two pair of Old Testament examples (vv 4-5, 6-8) are pre-

sented as proof that the Lord has indeed been active in rescu-
ing the godly (v 9a) and keeping the unrighteous for punishment until the day of judgment (vv 9b-10a).

4-5—In the first illustration, God's not sparing either the sinful angels before the Flood or the ancient world during the
Flood, is contrasted to his preserving righteous Noah and his
family. Here the sequence of events contained in Jude 5b-6 is
inverted so as to coincide with the chronology of Gen. 6:1-4
(angels) and 6:5—8:22 (sinful world, Flood, Noah). On the
tradition concerning the sinful angels and the role of the Flood
in Christian instruction see the comments on 1 Peter 3:19-21
and Jude 6. The phrase **cast them into hell** (v 4) renders a
Greek verb, *tartarōsas,* which occurs only here in the Greek
Bible. Literally it means "holding (them) captive in Tartarus."
According to Greek cosmology, Tartarus was a subterranean
place below Hades where evil people were committed and
punished after death. Use of this term in 2 Peter represents
still another instance of the author's blending of Jewish and
Greek world views.

Noah, in the estimation of Jews and Christians, was an exem-
plary, righteous man (Ezek. 14:14; 1 Peter 3:20), an heir of
righteousness (Heb. 11:7), a herald of repentance (Sibylline
Oracles 1.128; 1 Clement 7:6). He was a popular figure in
early Christian catacomb art. In 2 Peter he, like **righteous Lot**
(v 7), prepares as a **herald** the **way of righteousness** which true
believers are to follow (2:21; cf 3:13), in contrast to the unrighteous who take the errant route of Balaam (2:15-16).

6-8—The second example compares the condemnation of
Sodom and Gomorrah (v 6) to that of the angels (v 4) and
contrasts this divine punishment to God's rescue of Lot whose
righteousness is given double emphasis (vv 7, 8). On the significance of Sodom and Gomorrah for the early Christian community, see the comment on Jude 7. Lot, like Noah, is an example of God's rescue of the righteous. The combined reference
to Noah, the two cities, and Lot occurs elsewhere in the New

Testament only in Luke 17:26-30, a passage that also stresses the dissolute behavior that immediately precedes the coming of the final day (in Luke the day of the Son of Man).

9-10a—The conclusion of these "if" clauses (vv 4, 5, 6, 7) is now drawn. If, as we know, all this is a matter of historical record, **then the Lord** (whether God or Jesus Christ is left unspecified) **knows how to rescue** (as he did Lot, v 7) **the godly** (among whom the readers are included, see 1:3, 6; 3:11) **from trial** (i.e. the pressures exerted by the false teachers similar to the wicked who vexed Lot, v 8). He likewise knows how to **keep the unrighteous under punishment** (as he does the angels, v 4; see also 2:17; 3:7) **until the day of judgment** (3:7, 10, 12). Verse 10a combines elements of Jude 7, 8, and 16 (see the comments there) and prepares for the application of these examples to the false teachers. That which **especially** characterizes these unrighteous people is their despising of **authority** (see 2:1) and their following (the same verb as in 3:3; RSV: **indulge**) not the way of righteousness but the self-serving, unholy way of corruption (see 1:4; 2:18).

10b-22—From the predictive future tense the author now shifts to the descriptive present as he depicts the insolence, ignorance, divisiveness, and vacuousness of the apostates who ravaged the community.

10b-11—Here material from Jude is adopted and altered (cp Jude 8b-10a) to show how **bold and wilful** the false teachers are. To flaunt their freedom and superiority they **revile the glorious ones** (apparently the angels of v 4 are meant; cp. the text of Jude, and see the comment there). Yet even the angels who are superior to these persons do not presume to utter such a **reviling judgment** (the object of which is unclear here; see Jude 9).

12-13a—**But these** (persons), the author continues, are not the wise teachers they claim to be. Through an embellished version of Jude 10 (see the comment there), the author stresses their animal-like ignorance, their inevitable destruction (**born**

to be caught and killed, destroyed in the same destruction with
them) and their just retribution. By doing wrong ("being unrighteous" as in 2:9) they earn the reward of their wrongdoing.

13b—Jude's description (v 12) of carousing at the eucharistic
banquets is modified here. Revelling in the daytime they reckon
as *pleasure*. This is a further indication that the dissidents have
come under the influence of the Epicureans for whom pleasure
was the chief goal of life. Dissolute pursuit of this goal, however, had made **pleasure** *(hedōnē* in Greek) a pretext for hedonism. **Blots and blemishes** symbolizes their profanation of the
holy meal. Instead of the term "love feasts" *(agapais,* Jude 12)
however, 2 Peter substitutes, perhaps sarcastically, the term
dissipations *(apatais).* The similarity between these two Greek
terms suggests an intentional pun. The carousers had transformed love feasts into lascivious love-ins.

14—Hyperbole abounds here also. The false teachers have
eyes constantly on the lookout for occasions to sin. Continu-
ously enticing (as in vv 3, 18) **unsteady souls** (i.e. unstable persons) like themselves (3:16), they practice their skills (RSV:
train) **in greed** (see 2:3). **Accursed children** reformulates the
verdict of Jude's "woe to them" (v 11).

15-16—Since greed is a major vice of these teachers (vv 3,
14), greedy Balaam is the Old Testament example on which the
author focuses. Instead of proceeding on **the right way** (see
vv 2, 21), they strayed after the prophet-for-profit. This notorious character (see the comment on Jude 11) **loved gain from
wrongdoing** (the same phrase as in v 13a) and defied God (see
Num. 22:21-35). His dumb animal, however, possessed more
prophetic insight than did Balaam and even rebuked him for
his transgression. The verse implies that these avaricious teachers are of the same stripe as this mad prophet.

17-22—Finally the false teachers are attacked as vacuous
apostates who cannot deliver what they promise.

17—They are springs without water and flimsy **mists** dissi-
pated by a storm, empty and unstable. The remainder of this

verse loses the original sense it had in Jude 13. The "gloom of darkness" was the place reserved for the wandering stars (see the comment on Jude 13). Here the clause is related incongruously with springs and mists to assert again, however, the doom of the false teachers.

18-22—Uttering bombastic words of vanity (see Jude 16), they **entice** (see 2:3, 14; 3:17) converts who have **barely escaped from those who live in error** (i.e. those of the non-Christian society, cf. 1:4). Their bait is the promise of freedom for indulging in the **licentious passions of the flesh,** a teaching they implied came from Paul (see 3:15-16). But this turns the doctrine of Christian freedom on its head and entangles its proponents in an old form of bondage. Christian freedom is escape from the defilements of the world's corruption through the knowledge of the world's Savior (1:3-4). To be free as a Christian is to be a **slave** like Peter (1:1); not of **corruption** (v 20; cf. v 12) but of the **Master** who paid the price of his own life in order to free humans to be holy (2:1). By allowing themselves to be **overcome, entangled,** and **overpowered** by lust, greed and self-indulgence, these teachers are no longer free but slaves; their promise of freedom is therefore vacuous.

21-22—Better it were that they had never known **the way of righteousness** than that they should have turned away from **the holy commandment.** This holy commandment may, as in John 13:34 and 15:12, refer to Christ's command of love. Probably, however, the entirety of Christian truth and morality is intended (i.e. that "delivered to the saints" cf. Jude 3; also 1 Tim. 6:14; 1 John 2–5; 2 John.

This denunciation reaches its climax with an appeal to common wisdom (see Prov. 26:11 and the combination of dogs and swine in Matt. 7:6). Verse 22 compares the defection from holiness to the habits of unclean (unholy) animals. For Jews and Christians, the dog and the swine were the most despicable of creatures and hence symbolic of the Gentile enemies of God and his people (Deut. 14:8; Phil. 3:2; Rev. 22:15). In secular circles behaving like hedonistic pigs was a charge often leveled against the Epicureans and their sympathizers. Both implications fit the apostates. As the dog returns to its vomit and the washed sow to its mire, so these licentious backsliders demonstrate by their conduct their true identity. They are indeed irrational brutes (v 22 echoing v 12).

3:1-13   *I remind you again: contrary to the skepticism of the scoffers, the coming of the Lord is certain.*

Chapter 2 described how the false teachers denied the Lord's power and authority with their defiant behavior. Now the author takes up the issue of their scoffing at the Lord's coming. Following an introductory reference back to the themes of 1:12-21 (vv 1-2), objections raised to the coming of the Lord are refuted (vv 3-7), reason for its supposed delay is given (vv 8-9), and implications of its bearing on Christian behavior are stated (vv 10-13).

1-2—As stressed already at the beginning of this major section, it is urgent that the **beloved** (see 3:14, 17) **remember** (v 2; cf. 1:12-15) the reliable words of **the holy prophets** (1:19-21) and **your apostles** (1:16-18) concerning the **commandment of the Lord** (see 2:21 and the comment there). **This is now the second letter** could be a reference to a letter no longer extant; 1 Peter, however, was probably meant. Nevertheless, the description of its content (**in both . . .**) repeats the content of Jude (vv 17-18) rather than that of 1 Peter.

3-7—Verse 4 quotes the objections of the false teachers to the thought of the Lord's coming and vv 5-7 refute these objections in reverse order. First it is noted (v 3), however, that skepticism concerning this event should not take the readers by surprise. Ironically the appearance of scoffers (see Jude 18 and the comment there) and other "pseudo" types (see the comment on 2:1) is an inevitable accompaniment of the very eschatological events they themselves deny. Furthermore, such scoffing is linked with a thoroughly selfish and self-destructive way of life **(following their own passions)**, as indicated previously in 2:1-22.

Their position (v 4) flies in the face of observable fact. The scoffers claim that because nothing ever has changed **from the beginning of creation** nothing ever will change. Thus the idea of a divine coming is no more than a vulgar myth (1:16). The scoffing teachers, arguing like Epicureans from the theory of a static, immutable universe, hold that any idea of divine "interference" in human affairs is irrational and nonsensical. Human beings, therefore, are free to pursue pleasure as they choose without any concern for divine judgment after death. The latter point of this theory is refuted in vv 10-13. Verses 5-7, however, first cite two related facts concerning God's action in history that the scoffers deliberately **ignore.**

The dynamic **word** (v 5) by which God created the heavens and earth (see Gen. 1:6-10) and controlled the **water** (v 6) which eventually **deluged** an evil world (see Gen. 6:5—7:24, recalled in 2:5) is the **same word** (v 7) by which the present heavens and earth are **stored up for fire** at the end time and **kept until the day of judgment and destruction.** The imagery (water, fire), cosmic scope (heavens, earth, humans) and temporal perspective (end time resembles primordial time) is that of Jewish and Christian apocalyptic (teaching regarding God's final self-revelation). To refute the novel rationalism of the opponents, the author appeals to the venerable traditions in which the idea of God's coming among his creatures was first formulated.

Parousia, the Greek term for **coming** used here (v 4 and 1:16; 3:12) could denote the approach of any person, the visit of a special dignity or ruler, or even the epiphany of a god. In Christian vocabulary, however, it was used predominantly as a reference to the imminent coming of the exalted Lord Jesus Christ in his heavenly glory at the end of history (see Matt. 24:3, 27, 37, 39; 1 Cor. 15:23; 1 Thess. 2:19; 3:13; 4:15;

5:23; 2 Thess. 2:1, 8; James 5:7-8; 1 John 2:28). This coming of
the Messiah, not in the meekness of his earthly life but in the
full power of his heavenly exaltation, it was believed, would
accompany the coming of God himself. Thus the language
with which the Jewish people once described God's coming
became the terminology for depicting Christ's final advent as
well. Associated with this **coming of the day of God** (3:12) or
day of the Lord (3:10) were

- the entrance into the **kingdom** (1:11);
- the dawning of light (1:19) as prefigured in the transfiguration (1:17-18);
- the announcement of the coming (*kerygma* in Greek) through a **herald** (*keryx*, 2:5);
- the **day of judgment** (2:9; 3:7) when the righteous would be vindicated and the ungodly destroyed (2:3, 4-9, 12, 17; 3:7, 9, 11);
- the dissolution of the universe (3:7, 10, 12); and
- the inauguration of **new heavens and a new earth in which righteousness dwells** (3:13).

For all of these associations there are abundant examples
throughout the rest of the New Testament.

2 Peter not only draws heavily on this common apocalyptic
tradition. It also regards the event on which this tradition focuses, namely God's final coming in judgment and deliverance,
as an indispensable ingredient of authentic Christian faith and
the chief motivation for Christian morality. Confidence in the
parousia of God and his Messiah was part of a more embracing conviction of God's just rule of the cosmos and fatherly care of his creatures. To question the former was to doubt
the latter. From old creation to new creation, from H_2O to
holocaust, from primordial flood to final conflagration, 2 Peter
affirms that God will continue to be active in human history
as the Author of creation and Judge of righteousness.

8-9—Two things should not be ignored regarding the fulfillment of God's promised coming (v 4; see also 1:4; 3:13). First (v 8), God's measure of time does not conform to the human calendar: **one day** with the Lord **is as a thousand years.** This is the first recorded attempt on the part of Christians to explain the delay of the parousia through the use of Ps. 90:4 and the application of "sacred mathematics." When later taken literally by the millennialists, this thought ironically was used to support the very calculation of time which 2 Peter attempted to discourage. Second (v 9), God's apparent slowness by human standards is rather a manifestation of his generous forbearance toward all his creatures, thereby allowing sufficient time for the repentance of all (see Jonah 4:2; Rom. 2:4; 9:22; 1 Peter 3:20).

10-13—The coming **day of the Lord** and the cosmic dissolution it entails has present moral implications. Since this day will come as unexpectedly **as a thief** (v 10; see the same eschatological simile in Matt. 24:43; Luke 12:39; 1 Thess. 5:2), and **since all these things** (i.e. heavens, elements of the universe, earth, and human deeds) will be judged, you readers ought to lead **lives of holiness and godliness** (echoing 1:5-11). The notion of a final conflagration of all that exists (vv 7, 10-12) occurs nowhere else in the Bible but is in keeping with Greek thought. The association of fire with the day of the Lord and final judgment (as in Zeph. 1:18; Isa. 66:15-18; Mal. 4:1) made possible the eventual blending of Jewish and Greek imagery (see 1 Enoch 1:6-7; Sibylline Oracles 3.71-92; 4.171-78). The present moment is an opportunity to await patiently the promise of new heavens and a new earth filled with righteousness, and to hasten that day by holy and godly living (see Isa. 65:17; 66:22; Rev. 21:1). This latter idea reflects the similar conviction in Judaism that if God's people were but once to repent and faithfully keep the commandments, the Messiah would appear (see also Acts 3:19-20).

■ *3:14-18 Wait for the Lord in grace and knowledge, in peace and holiness.*

The concluding exhortation of the **beloved** (vv 14, 17)
— repeats the call to patience and holiness (vv 14-15a),
— cites a distortion of Paul's proclamation as another example of the error of the false teachers (vv 15b-16),
— warns against being carried away by this error (v 17),
— encourages stability through continued growth in grace and knowledge (v 18a), and
— ends with a brief doxology (v 18b).

14-15a—Because the beloved have these things to look forward to (referring back to vv 10-13), they, therefore, must make every effort (see 1:10, 15) to be found pure and at peace with God when he comes to judge the world. **To be found** means to be judged by God as having **no spot or blemish** (see 1 Peter 1:19 and Jude 24 and the comment there) in contrast to the false teachers, those **blots and blemishes** (2:13) whose works will be **found** guilty by God (3:10; see Psalms of Solomon 17:10 for a similar usage). **Count the forbearance of our Lord as salvation** restates the point of v 9. The final judgment has not yet occurred because a merciful God desires the repentance and salvation of all his creatures.

15b-16—**Our beloved brother Paul** wrote nothing different from what we say. The apostolic witness is a unified one. This specific reference to Paul, his several letters and their equation with the **other scriptures** are important indications of the late date of 2 Peter. The Pauline writings, originally addressed to separate localities, have been collected and are on their way to being recognized together with the other scriptures as equally sacred and normative, a process pointing to the late first and early second centuries. This reference to Paul also indicates the main authority to whom the false teachers appealed for their peculiar concept of Christian freedom. Thus the phrase **speaking of this as he does in all his letters** (v 16a) no doubt embraces not only Paul's teaching concerning divine forbearance and the urgency of repentance (see Rom. 2:4-11; 9:19-29; 1 Tim. 1:16) but also his stress on the moral integrity that Christian freedom involves (see Rom. 6–8; 1 Cor. 7, 9; Gal. 3-6). The false teachers of 2 Peter, like earlier converts who misconstrued the teachings of Paul (e.g. Rom. 3:8; 6:1, 12-23; 15:1; 1 Cor. 5:9-13; 6:12; 10:23; 2 Cor. 6:8; Gal. 5:13-25), distort Paul's message just as they do **the other scriptures** (see 1:19-21). Granted, **some things in them** are **hard to understand;** Paul himself conceded as much (e.g. 1 Cor. 2:14–3:4). Nonetheless, the **ignorant and unstable** apostates (2:12, 19-22) who **twist** his and other sacred words in order to justify their own private opinions and passions (1:20; 2:15, 22; 3:3) do so **to their own destruction** (see 2:1, 3, 9, 12, 17; 3:7, 10).

17-18—Therefore the readers, supplied with Peter's warning in advance (see 1:12-15), must **beware** ("be on guard") lest they too be carried away by the waywardness (RSV: **error;** see Jude 11) of such unprincipled (**lawless,** cf. 2:1) **men** and thereby lose their **own stability.** Maintenance of this stability, with which the letter as a whole is urgently concerned, is possible, however, by growing in the **grace** (as in 1:2) **and knowledge of our Lord and Savior Jesus Christ** which the readers have already received as a divine gift (1:3-11). The letter thus concludes on the themes with which it began: the urgency of continued growth in the divine gifts that have set Christians apart from a corrupt world, and of continued confidence in the divine promises of an eternal reward.

The features which set 2 Peter apart from the rest of the New Testament likewise continue through the very end of the letter. The doxology with which it concludes (v 18b) is but a fragment of the elaborate formulation of Jude (vv 24-25). Of more interest, however, are the object of that blessing and the phrase, **day of eternity.** Except for 2 Tim. 4:18, this is the only certain instance in the New Testament of a doxology addressed to Jesus Christ (God being the usual object of such blessings). This corresponds to the unusual degree to which Jesus Christ and God are associated and virtually identified in this letter. Both are designated as **Savior** (1:1, 11; 2:20; 3:2; see 3:15); both are **divine** (1:3, 4); and the coming **day** involves the advent, glory, and action of both (1:17-18, 19; 2:8, 9; 3:3, 7, 8, 10, 12, 18). 2 Peter thus embarks on the path taken by later generations toward an increasing stress on Jesus Christ's divinity and his role in the divine rule of the cosmos. The phrase **day of eternity** is also unique in the New Testament (see Sirach 18:10). Concluding a letter which has laid such emphasis on the **day of the Lord,** it expresses one last time the everlasting duration of that day of righteousness which was depicted at the outset of the letter by the equally unique phrase, **eternal kingdom** (1:11).

Through its extraordinary blending of Greek cultural expression and Jewish and Christian apocalyptic tradition, this final letter of the New Testament represents a valiant effort on the part of the post-apostolic church to remain faithful to its ancient heritage in the midst of conflict and change. Regardless of how Christianity accommodates itself to the Greek experience, 2 Peter affirms that the object of Christian hope and the motivation of Christian morality must remain intact. The tradition preserved in the letter is a precious gift to later generations of the Petrine heritage. Its vital concern for the unity, stability, and integrity of the church gives the message of 2 Peter an enduring significance.

JUDE

John H. Elliott

INTRODUCTION

The history of the Letter of Jude in the Christian church generally has been one of benign neglect. Soon after its appearance it was incorporated into the letter of 2 Peter (see the Commentary on 2 Peter) and by the end of the second century it was regarded, along with other Catholic Epistles, as canonical at Rome, Carthage, and Alexandria. In the following centuries, however, it fell under suspicion (e.g. Eusebius and Jerome), probably because of its use of apocryphal writings which were themselves rejected as non-canonical (vv 9, 14-15). Later still, in 1523, Luther considered it "nothing more than an epistle directed against our clerics, bishops, priests, and monks" and the ecclesiastical abuses of his own day (*Luther's Works,* vol. 30, p. 203). His doubts about its authorship and his opinion that it "need not be counted among the chief books which are supposed to lay the foundations of the faith" (Ibid., vol. 35, p. 398) have been shared by many in the church ever since. Jude has been excluded from most lectionaries and is thus rarely read in the liturgy; seldom, if ever, is it a focus of preaching or Bible study.

Nevertheless, its inclusion in the canon of sacred scripture testifies to the great importance the church once attached—and should continue to attach—to this letter's concern for moral conduct as well as doctrinal orthodoxy. According to Jude, Christian behavior, no less than Christian belief, is a hallmark of the **faith once for all delivered to the saints.** Jude, like the epistle of James whose moral outlook it so closely resembles, preserves for Christianity the ethical heritage of Judaism and the indispensability of a faith active in love. Such writings reveal the earnestness with which the words of the Lord were taken in early Christianity; namely that it is by deeds and not simply words that the Christian will be known and judged (Matt. 7:15-27; 25:31-46).

With its condemnatory tone and minimal expression of good news the Letter of Jude, it must be granted, offers a rather limited basis for Christian devotion and celebration. Its stress on unity, fidelity to the faith, and moral integrity, however, assures for the letter a perennial relevance. In this light the brief Letter of Jude and its role in the canon perhaps deserves more attention than it has generally been accorded.

1. Literary Type and Composition

Jude has the appearance rather than the full form of a letter, lacking a proper conclusion and containing only a general address (v 1). It is a literary composition reflecting the influence of both Jewish and Greek culture. The Jewish influence is seen in the predominantly moral focus of Jude, its heavy use of examples drawn from the Old Testament and other Jewish writings (vv 5-7, 9, 11, 14-15) and its reference to the end of time (v 18). The Greek influence is seen in its vocabulary, style, and in the allusions in vv 13 and 23. In its form, general address, focus, and mixed cultural character, it closely resembles the Letter of James. The similarities concern form more than specific content, however, and therefore they present no case for literary dependency, as in the case of Jude and 2 Peter. The resemblances between Jude and James, nevertheless, do suggest, if not a common place of origin, at least a common cultural and religious background. This would certainly be likely if, as seems to be the case, the James to whom the author of Jude is a brother (v 1) is the same James to whom the letter of James is ascribed (James 1:1).

A notable literary feature of Jude is the frequent use of triplets or triads (vv 1, 2 etc.) and the development of thought through the use of link-words (e.g. **beloved, love, beloved,** vv 1, 2, 3) which establish the continuity and unity of the argument.

A series of comparisons and contrasts mark the overall structure of the letter. The present intruders (v 4) against whom Jude inveighs are *compared* with notorious examples from the past. The **beloved** (vv 1, 3, 17, 20) addressees, on the other hand, are *contrasted* to these evil persons. These comparisons and contrasts dramatize the divisions within the community (vv 12, 19) and illustrate the distinctions between the godly and the ungodly. The situation calls for a drawing of lines between "us and them" (although excommunication is not proposed, as in 1 Cor. 5:6, 11). The unity of the community and the integrity of its faith (v 4) is at stake. Compromise and further collusion with the ungodly is out of the question. The beloved are rather to **contend for the faith once for all delivered to the saints.**

The unspecific nature of the letter's address (vv 1-2) is matched by the lack of personal references throughout and by the absence of personal greetings at its close (as also James, 2 Peter, and 1 John). The letter concludes, rather, with a full liturgical doxology (cp. 2 Peter 3:18) praising God the Savior through Jesus Christ for the dominion and power by which he preserves the faithful.

2. Situation and Strategy

Originally the author had intended to write to the addressees a positive, confirming letter regarding **our common salvation** (v 3a); that is, the hope of salvation uniting believers from both Jewish and pagan backgrounds. The outbreak of a disruptive crisis, however, threatened this unity, and necessitated a shift from irenical to polemical tone (v 4).

Certain converts to the Christian community (vv 4, 12) lacking an accurate understanding of the faith and its moral obligations (v 10) were not only disrupting and dividing the community but distorting and denying the very basis of Christian faith itself. Confusing the liberty which divine grace confers with a license to self-indulgence, sexual promiscuity, rejection of authority, and exploitation of other believers, they denied with their behavior that Jesus Christ is **our only Master and Lord** (vv 4, 8, 12, 16, 18). Apparently claiming for themselves a superior knowledge and gift of the Spirit (disputed in vv 8, 10, 18), which supposedly elevated them above conventional morality, they had divided the community by enticing others to side with them.

Claims to special knowledge *(gnosis* in Greek) and spiritual superiority coupled with libertine behavior, typifies the various Gnostic heretical groups which were organized and condemned from the second century onward. However, the absence in Jude of the key term *gnosis,* and of any trace of a developed theology or organization of the trouble-makers, indicates that they were similar to the converts who created problems in earlier phases of the Christian mission (see esp. 1 Cor. and Col.; also Rom. 16:17-18; Eph. 4:14; 5:6; Phil. 3:18-19; 2 Thess. 3:2-3; Rev. 2–3).

The situation in Jude is an example of a critical problem with which the Christian movement had to deal. Its proclamation of the universality of God's grace and its inclusion of converts from diverse cultural, social, and religious origins contributed greatly toward the rapid advance of the movement, but it also contained the seeds of potential friction. There was, therefore, an ongoing need to clarify the features of Christian unity amid such diversity. Diversity, combined with temporal distance from the initial formation of the Christian movement, created the need for unifying norms.

In the initial apostolic age (ending roughly by A.D. 70), disciples, eye-witnesses, and apostles called by Christ were the authoritative witnesses to the gospel and the personal guarantors of its truth. In the years following, believers of later generations collected and recalled this authoritative witness. Evangelists gathered and preserved the words and deeds of the Lord and perceived in his teaching a message for their own age. Disciples of the apostles likewise recorded the teachings of their leaders. In similar fashion the author of Jude looks back to the apostolic age and appeals to the **predictions of the apostles** (v 17) and **the faith once for all delivered to the saints** (v 4) which, along with the testimony of scripture (vv 5b-16), provides the norm necessary for determining authentic Christian belief and behavior. According to this standard the disturbers of the community stood condemned and for this faith the beloved were to earnestly contend.

The strategy of the letter thus involves a combination of recollection and repudiation. The author engages not in debate but in denunciation. Jude's aim is to identify and expose the troublemakers, insulate the faithful, and thereby insure confidence, commitment, and order among the faithful. The dissidents, according to Jude, are **ungodly persons** (vv 4, 15, 18) who have secretly joined the community under the pretense of conversion (v 4). But when they are examined in the light of what the readers already know, their masquerade becomes self-evident. They are just like the iniquitous peoples and persons of old (5b-7, 11). They defile the flesh in their dreamings (v 8), deride what they fail to understand (v 10), disrupt the love feasts (v 12), deceive by appearance (vv 12-13), deviate from the true course (v 13), divide the community and are devoid of the Spirit (v 19). Their end, too, is divine destruction (v 10). By history (vv 5b-11) and prophecy (vv 14-16) they stand condemned. These **scoffers** were also anticipated by the apostles as signals of the end of time (v 18). Therefore, their divisive behavior should come as no surprise. They distort

God's grace and **deny our only Master and Lord, Jesus Christ** (v 4).

The faithful, therefore, are to **build yourselves up on your holy faith, pray in the Holy Spirit, keep yourselves in the love of God,** and **wait for the mercy of our Lord Jesus Christ** (vv 20-21). Such commitment will enable the beloved to rescue some of their vascillating brothers and sisters (v 23). In this life-and-death struggle the faithful may be sure of the power of God to keep them from failing or falling (vv 24-25).

3. Origin, Destination, and Date

The author, as Luther also noted, was not an apostle and therefore was not the Jude mentioned in Luke 6:16 and Acts 1:13. Nor does the author claim to be such since he refers to the apostles as a group distinct from himself (v 17) and identifies himself rather as **a servant of Jesus Christ and brother of James** (v 1). The most prominent James in the early church was the blood brother of the Lord who, after Peter and until his own death in A.D. 62, was the influential leader of the "mother church" in Jerusalem and probably the person implied in James 1:1. If **brother** in Jude 1 figuratively means a brother-in-the-faith or ministerial co-worker, as it frequently does in the New Testament, then the person implied in Jude 1 could have been Jude (Judas) Barsabbas, a "prophet" of the Jerusalem community and co-worker of James (Acts 15:22-34).

Since little else is recorded of this Jude, however, it is more likely that in v 1 the blood brother of James (and of the Lord) is meant. That this Jude actually *wrote* the letter is improbable on several counts. Judging from its literary style and vocabulary the letter was composed by a Hellenistic-Jewish Christian which Jude, the brother of Jesus and James, certainly was not. The problem cited in the letter, furthermore, suggests a mixed cultural milieu beyond the environs of Palestine proper where Jude lived and worked. And the reference to **the predictions of** the apostles (v 17) scarcely seems natural for one who could speak authoritatively on the basis of his *own* experiences if he were actually the brother of Jesus and James.

It therefore seems probable that the letter was attributed to Jude but actually composed within the circle of Christians allied with both brothers. The similarity between the letters ascribed to each of these brothers makes this common origin all the more plausible. The letter was written in Jude's name with stress on his relation to James because of the authority and continuing veneration of these men and the family of the Lord in the early church. They represented personal links with the historical Jesus and the apostolic age.

The actual place of composition, destination, and date of the letter are very uncertain. The area of Syria or northern Palestine is perhaps most likely. Jude and James were at least known to the Christians of northern Palestine and Syria. There a letter on their authority would have weight, and there the traditions Jude cites would have been known. There too, especially in Syria and Antioch, was the cultural mix of Jewish and Gentile Christians which precipitated the problem treated in the letter. As Paul's letters attest, the mission in Asia Minor encountered similar problems. However, it is not so clear that there the authority of Jude would have carried as much weight.

Dealing with internal as well as external problems by referring to the apostolic age or to earlier predictions and teaching is a characteristic of the later New Testament writings (c. A.D. 70-100). The use of this strategy of recollection and its explicit encouragement in verses 5 and 17-18 would situate Jude within this later period. If written within the first decade or so of this period (i.e., 70-80), its actual composition by Jude, James' brother, still remains a remote, though unlikely, possibility.

OUTLINE OF JUDE

Evidence concerning the outline of Jude has been discussed above in connection with its literary type and composition. The letter opens with a salutation (vv 1-2) and concludes with a benediction (vv 24-25). Verses 3-4 state the purpose and occasion of the exhortation and 5a and 17 introduce two sections (vv 5-16, 17-23) calling the readers to remembrance. Within these units the **beloved** (vv 3, 17, 20-23) are contrasted to the dissidents (vv 4, 8, 10, 11a, 12, 16, 19) who are compared to **ungodly persons** known or anticipated from of old (vv 5b-7, 11b, 14-16, 18). This yields the following outline:

1-2 *Jude, slave of Jesus Christ and brother of James to the Beloved: Greeting!*

3-4 *Beloved, contend for the faith, mindful of devious intruders in your midst.*

5-16 *By way of my reminder, compare these ungodly persons with those of the past who were also objects of God's judgment.*

17-23 *Beloved, in contrast to these ungodly people, re-*

*member the apostles' warnings and be firm in your
faith.*

24-25   *Praise be to God who will keep you spotless and
secure.*

COMMENTARY

1-2   Salutation: Jude, slave of Jesus Christ and brother of James to the Beloved: Greeting!

Detail concerning the author is not balanced by equally specific information regarding the addressees, their identity or location. With the exception of 1 Peter, this typifies the so-called "Catholic Epistles" among which Jude is included (James, 1-2 Peter, 1-2-3 John, Jude). Of the five Christians bearing this common Jewish name in the New Testament, the Jude (Judas) meant here is in all likelihood the **brother of James,** the renowned leader of the Jerusalem church. Both were younger brothers of Jesus (Matt. 13:55/Mark 6:3) and later played influential roles in the eastern theater of the Christian movement (see Section 3 of the Introduction). **Servant/slave of Jesus Christ** was a formulation adopted from the Old Testament "servant of God" and associated especially with those who ministered in the Lord's service. The double identification establishes the authority of the author and his message as well as his subordination as "slave" to the authority of his **Master and Lord** (cf. v 4; also vv 17, 21, 25).

The addressees are described but not specifically identified. The specific nature of the problem troubling them, however, rules out the likelihood that the letter was intended for Christians at large. **Called, beloved, kept** (v 1), as the triad of terms in v 2 and the triad of exhortations in vv 21-22, express the origin, basis, and goal of Christian existence and thus the motive and means for heeding the exhortation to follow.

Within the New Testament, the greeting (v 2) is a unique formulation but bears close similarity to that in 1 Peter 1:2 and 2 Peter 1:2. In the second century it appears in slightly expanded form in the salutations of two letters sent by the Christians of Smyrna in the province of Asia (Polycarp to the Philippians and the Martyrdom of Polycarp).

3-4   *Beloved, contend for the faith, mindful of devious intruders in your midst.*

Originally intending to write irenically about **our common salvation,** the author suddenly found it necessary to confront a problem that endangered the unifying bond of experience and faith (v 3). In v 4 the danger is briefly summarized and evaluated.

The address, **beloved** (v 3 and vv 17, 20), expresses the affection among believers which God's love engenders and is related to a similar term by which the Christian eucharist was called, namely **love feast** (v 12). **Our common salvation** and **faith** likewise express here in summary fashion that which unites all believers (Jewish and Gentile Christians as well as Jude and his audience). **Salvation** (*sōtēria* in Greek) and savior *(sōtēr)* were terms often used in Greek culture to describe rescue from a perilous situation through persons or deities endowed with extraordinary powers (such as rulers, public benefactors, and physicians, especially those devoted to Asclepius Soter, the god of healing). This terminology was adopted by Christians to proclaim God's extraordinary deliverance of his people through the new Savior, Jesus Christ (see v 23; also Luke 2:11; Acts 13:23; Phil. 3:20). In Jude, **salvation** depicts the past (v 5) as well as the present (v 3, 23) experience of God's people.

As **salvation** summarizes the experience of divine rescue in

Jude, so the term **faith** (vv 3, 20) embraces all that Christians believe, teach, and confess. Rather than referring to the act of believing (its predominant usage in the New Testament), faith here designates that which is believed, the doctrines to which assent is given. "The once-for-all-delivered-to-the-saints faith" is presented here as something definitively formed and fixed long ago and **delivered** intact down to the present hour. Thus faith here is identical to sacred tradition. While this objective sense of the term is occasionally found in earlier New Testament writings (Rom. 10:8; Gal. 1:23; 6:10), such a usage is typical of a later age concerned with the consolidation and normative function of proclamation, creed, and instruction for the purpose of refuting error within the community. This meaning of faith here in Jude thus suggests that it is one of the later compositions of the New Testament.

The verb, **contend** (occurring only here in the New Testament), is related in its Greek root *(agon-)* to language pertaining to Greek athletic competitions and contests waged in honor of the gods. Such terminology and imagery was adopted by the Christians to depict the self-discipline and struggle the service of God required (1 Cor. 9:24-27; 1 Tim. 6:12; 2 Tim. 4:7; Heb. 12:1). **Saints** was a designation for all who were sanctified by God in contrast to the unclean outsiders (see the commentary on 1 Peter 1:14-16) but it was particularly used in reference to the Jerusalem community (Rom. 15:25, 26, 31; 1 Cor. 16:1, 15; 2 Cor. 8:4; 9:1).

The readers were to contend for the faith because it was being distorted and denied by deceptive intruders. Certain persons had "wormed their way in" (NEB) by stealth and pretense. This verb also occurs only here in the New Testament but closely resembles Paul's description of similar false brethren in Galatia who secretly "slipped in to spy out our freedom which we have in Christ Jesus" (Gal. 2:4). Appearing to have embraced the faith and taking part in the love feasts (v 12), they were in reality **ungodly persons** (i.e., thoroughly irreverent and opposed to God's will; see v 18 and the repetition of this term in v 15). Like the sinners of old (vv 5-7, 11, 14-15) they too were **designated for this** (similar) **condemnation.** For they **pervert the grace of our God** (which liberates the children of God, Rom. 8:21; 2 Cor. 3:17) **into licentiousness.** Licentiousness, like ungodliness, summarizes their insolent and disobedient behavior. It often is used, however, in connection with sexual immorality in particular (e.g., Rom. 13:3; 2 Cor. 12:21; Gal. 5:19; cf. 2 Peter 2:7) and therefore perhaps directly anticipates vv 7-8.

Precisely how the dissidents **deny our only Master and Lord, Jesus Christ** is not stated. The immoral behavior mentioned already in this verse as well as throughout the letter is most likely the mode of denial by the ungodly persons. The identification of Jesus Christ as *both* **Master and Lord** is unique in the New Testament and seemingly redundant, unless a point is to be made through repetition. That point could concern the complete control that the Master and Lord exercises over his slaves (v 1; cf. Rom. 6:12-19). The ungodly, regarding the liberation from sin as the release from all control, **reject authority** (v 8), claim a status superior to that of even an archangel (vv 9-10), and pursue their own inclinations (vv 16, 18) even presuming to "shepherd themselves" (see the commentary on v 12). In so doing they are insubordinate also to their Master and assume for themselves a superiority which is the Lord's alone.

5-16 *By way of my reminder, compare these ungodly persons with those of the past who were also objects of God's judgment.*

In order to expose the real nature of the troublemakers and their impending condemnation, Jude recalls facts of which the readers were **once for all** (as in v 3) **fully informed** (v 5a). These lessons were drawn from the Old Testament and Jewish apocryphal writings which at Jude's time were still regarded as inspired and holy writings.

5-7—The three examples of the Israelite wilderness generation (v 5b), the rebellious angels (v 6), and the inhabitants of Sodom and Gomorrah (v 7) each concludes on the note Jude wishes most to stress: God's destruction (v 5b), judgment (v 6) and punishment (v 7) of evil types like the dissidents.

Verse 5b alludes to the events recorded in Num. 14:1-35 (cf. 32:10-15) which are also used as warnings to Christians in 1 Cor. 10:1-11 and Heb. 3:7—4:11. Even though God saved this people by liberating them from the power of the Egyptians, he also destroyed this generation in the wilderness because of their grumbling discontent and lack of trust in his continuing care.

Verse 6 recalls the popular tradition of the rebellious angels who in the period just prior to the great flood abandoned their celestial position and **proper dwelling** (i.e., heaven) and had intercourse with human women. The biblical basis of this story, Gen. 6:1-4, was extensively expanded in the Jewish apocryphal literature, esp. 1 Enoch (chs. 6-16), as an explanation of the origin of evil in the world and a warning against Jewish intercourse (social and sexual) with Gentiles. Christian reference to this tradition and the divine punishment of the angels occurs here and in 2 Peter 2:4, 9 as well as in 1 Peter 3:19 (see the commentary there for further detail). These disobedient spirits or angels would be bound in **eternal chains** in the **gloom** (darkness) of the second heaven (2 Enoch 7:1-3; Testament of Levi 3:2), until the **great day,** i.e., the final judgment (1 Enoch 10:6; cf. Acts 2:20; Rev. 6:17; 16:14).

Verse 7 refers to cities around the Dead Sea whose sudden destruction through fire had for centuries been regarded as a classic example of divine judgment. Lying on the Jordan fault, this region and its chief cities of Sodom and Gomorrah had been turned into an arid, infertile, and sulphurous wasteland around 1900 B.C. probably by an earthquake and an ensuing conflagration fed by the rich mineral deposits of the area. In Gen. 18-19 this devastation was interpreted as the result of God's punishment of the inhabitants for their sin of inhospitality and their attempt at intercourse with angels. Elsewhere in the Old Testament their destruction was attributed also to their barbarous administration of justice (Isa. 1:10; 3:9), their pride and luxuriousness (Ezek. 16:48-50; Sirach 16:8) or their ungodliness and deceit (Jer. 23:14). When Judaism in the postexilic age confronted an alien Greek culture and morality, these cities were used to symbolize foreign idolatry and a morality alien to God and his holy people (Jubilees 16:5-6; 20:5; Testament of Naphthali 3:4-5, etc.). Although Sodom eventually has been associated with homosexuality in particular (as in "sodomy" or "sodomite"), this association is typical neither of the Old Testament nor the New Testament. In the case of the latter as well as the former, Sodom is used to symbolize only divine judgment visited on evil people (Matt. 10:15; 11:23-24; Luke 10:12; 17:29; Rom. 9:29; 2 Peter 2:6; Rev. 11:8).

The sin on which Jude focuses is literally "pursuing other flesh" (than their own kind) as did the angels referred to in the preceding verse. The RSV translation, **indulged in unnatural lust,** misses this connection and fails to capture the implication of *other* flesh. As the angels joined with human flesh (bodies), so the human residents of Sodom and Gomorrah sought to join themselves to angels. The lesson for Jude's readers is that the dissidents in similar fashion **defile** their bodies (v 8) through physical (and perhaps sexual) association with sinners (a problem similar to that with which Paul dealt in 1 Cor. 5-6).

8—This verse makes the application. Despite these well-known warnings (vv 5b-7), **these men** (the **ungodly** of v 4) **in their dreamings** (a sarcastic put-down of their source of knowledge and inspiration) not only

- **defile** their bodies (those in vv 6-7) but
- **reject authority** ("lordship" in Greek) and

- **revile the glorious ones** (i.e., the obedient; cf. Heb. 9:5; Testament of Levi 18:5; Testament of Judah 25:2).

9—Here the author presents an instance with which the reviling in verses 8 and 10 is contrasted. The reference is to a legend regarding the burial of Moses (Deut. 34:6) which, according to the Church Fathers, Jude knew from the apocryphal document, *The Assumption of Moses*. The dissidents who revile the glorious angels are contrasted in their arrogance to the attitude of one of the most glorious of these angels, the archangel Michael (on Michael see also Dan. 10:13; 12:1; and Rev. 12:7). When, according to the legend, Michael contended with the devil for the body of Moses, which the devil claimed belonged to him (because Moses was a murderer), Michael **did not presume to pronounce a reviling judgment** on the devil but left that judgment to God saying only "The Lord rebuke you" (cf. Zech. 3:2).

10—The dreamers, by contrast, **revile** (as in v 8c) **whatever they do not understand** (regarding the dignity and superiority of angels and lordship) and where they claim to be knowledgeable (regarding their physical bodies, v 8a) they know no more than animals who act only on instinct and lack the distinctive human quality of reason. In so doing they are destroyed (see 2 Peter 2:10-13, 21-22 for an expansion on this line of thought).

11-16—Although they contain different points of comparison (Old Testament figures, v 11; natural phenomena, vv 12-13; Enoch's prophecy, vv 14-15), these verses form a single unit of thought. This unit begins and ends with the Greek verb for "conduct" *(poreuō)* which is translated **walk** in v 11 and **following** in v 16.

11—Rather than emulating Michael the archangel, the dissidents follow the path of those notorious reprobates Cain, Balaam, and Korah. The exclamation **woe!** intimates the judgment to befall them. Cain, in the Old Testament and later Jewish and Christian tradition, represented not only a murderer but an envious, greedy, and hateful person. He was a child of the evil one (1 John 3:12) who defied God and despised his brother. Balaam (cf. also 2 Peter 2:15-16) exemplified the sin of prophecy for profit (Num. 31:16). He too defied God and **for the sake of gain** hired himself out to curse God's people and lead them to apostasy (see Deut. 23:4-5; Neh. 13:1-3). The Christians at Pergamum in Asia Minor also followed his idolatrous ways (Rev. 2:14-15). The last of this terrible trio, Korah, led his 250 followers in a rebellion against Israel's divinely-appointed leaders, Moses and Aaron (Num. 16:1-35). God's response to such insubordination was total annihilation: "the earth opened its mouth and swallowed them up" (Num. 16:32). Woe to those who follow Cain's lead, who wallow in Balaam's deception (RSV: error) and perish in Korah's kind of rebellion!

12-13—The first half of v 12 denounces the disruptive behavior of these ungodly persons at the community meals; the remainder of vv 12 and 13 compares them with unproductive and uncontrolled elements of nature. The common meals eaten by Christians in connection with their liturgical commemoration of Christ Jesus' death and resurrection are here for the first time in the New Testament called **love feasts** (*agapai,* i.e., banquets of brotherly love; see also Ignatius, Letter to the Smyrnaeans 8:2, c. A.D. 110). 1 Cor. 11-14 attests not only the misunderstanding and selfishness which occasionally accompanied these meals but also the spirit of love (ch 13) which they were intended to express and foster. By feasting together (RSV: carouse) but lacking reverence for God and the Lord, and by **looking after themselves** (perhaps, like Korah, rejecting the authority of the community's shepherds), the disturbers were **blemishes** (the same Greek root as in "spotted," v 23) on the holy feast of love.

As **waterless clouds** and **fruitless trees** the deceivers were all show and no substance. They fail to produce what they promise (see Prov. 25:14; Matt. 21:18-19). **Twice dead,** without fruit and now without leaves and life-giving roots, they are only good for the fire (see Matt. 3:10; 7:19; Luke 13:6-9;

John 15:2-6; 2 Peter 3:4). As **wild waves** foam up the scum of
the sea, so these unholy persons churn up and pollute the
community with their shameful behavior (an image derived
from Isa. 57:20). As **wandering stars,** they were not only unstable and deceptive, but doomed for destruction. In Jude's
age the planets were regarded as stars which were not fixed
but "wandered" through the heavens (whence the term "planet"
from the Greek, "to wander," "to lead astray"). These seven
wandering stars were also associated with the angels who wandered from their heavenly home (see v 6) and led humankind
astray (1 Enoch 18-21). As these stars were condemned to the
nether gloom of darkness (as in v 6) for wandering from God
and not giving light, so also the deceivers in Jude's audience
will be condemned for wandering from the truth and causing
others to do likewise. Altogether the comparisons illustrate the
application of the Lord's moral principle: "You will know them
by their fruits" (Matt. 7:15-20; 24:45—25:46).

14-16—Explicit reference is made here (vv 14b-15 quoting
1 Enoch 1:9) to the writing on which much of the preceding
material was implicitly based. With this prophecy from Enoch
is coupled a final denunciation that completes the series of
comparisons begun in v 5.

To Enoch, the faithful patriarch of the seventh generation
of human history (Gen. 5:21-24), was attributed a writing which
actually was compiled in the second to first century before the
Common Era. This work, through a variety of detail and
imagery, dreams and visions which reflected the cosmology
and theology of postexilic Judaism, dealt with fundamental
issues concerning evil, its origin and present manifestations,
and the conflict between the godly and the ungodly, the divine
vindication of the former and condemnation of the latter. The
book was well known in Jewish (including Qumran) and Christian (especially apocalyptic) circles and exerted much influence
on the thought and literature of both religious communities.
(In the New Testament this includes not only Jude, but also the

Gospels, 1 Peter and Rev. if not more). In the early church, 1 Enoch was regarded by many as sacred scripture (e.g., The Epistle of Barnabas, Tertullian, Ethiopic Christianity); later in the fourth century, however, it was excluded from the canon.

Enoch's vision of the future (1 Enoch 1:2), related in the past prophetic tense, concerned God's final coming (1:3-6) in "judgment upon all men" (1:7). As he came "to make peace with the righteous" (1:8), so he came "to destroy all the ungodly," convicting them of their wicked deeds and words (1:9 quoted in Jude 14b-15). According to Jude this prophecy pertains precisely to these (v 14a) who now trouble his audience with their defiant ungodliness. Having previously (vv 5-13) described their ungodly *deeds,* Jude then applies Enoch's reference to **all the harsh things which the ungodly sinners have spoken against him** to their ungodly *words* (v 16).

Following their own selfish desires (like Cain, Balaam, and Korah, v 11), they are **grumblers** and **malcontents** similar to the dissatisfied and disbelieving Israelites in the wilderness (recalling v 5; see Num. 14:27-29. These two terms occur only here in the New Testament and are possibly derived from the Assumption of Moses 7:7). **Flattering people to gain** (personal) **advantage,** they attempt the same ploy condemned in James 2:1-9 and in the Assumption of Moses 5:5. By their ungodly words and deeds these impious frauds follow in the path of their notorious predecessors and therefore share in their condemnation and destruction.

17-23   *Beloved, in contrast to these ungodly people, remember the apostles' warnings and be firm in your faith.*

From an excoriation of the ungodly, Jude turns to an encouragement of the **beloved.** The lessons contained in the holy writings (vv 5-16) are reinforced by words (of warning) spoken beforehand (RSV: **predictions**) by the apostles. In contrast to the divisive pseudo-believers to whom the apostolic words apply, the beloved are urged to remember their roots and remain faithful.

17-18—The specific formulation of the apostles' eschatological warning (**In the last time . . .**) is recorded nowhere else in the New Testament except 2 Peter 3:3 which is dependent on this verse of Jude. A general theme in apostolic teaching rather than a particular saying is probably meant. The Gospels recall that the Lord himself had told beforehand of "false Christs and false prophets" who would arise and lead astray the elect (Matt. 24:23-28; Mark 13:21-23). The apostles likewise had spoken beforehand of possible distortions of the gospel (Gal. 1:9; 5:21; 2 Cor. 13:2; 1 Thess. 4:6) and of the advent of false teachers in the last days (Acts 20:29-30; 1 Tim. 4:1-3; 2 Tim. 3:1-5; 4:3). The use of the rare term, **scoffers,** which occurs only here and 2 Peter 3:3 in the New Testament and only in Isa. 3:4 (Greek) in the Old Testament, however, makes it likely that Jude sees the apostolic warning as linked to Isaiah's prophecy concerning the final "day of the Lord" when the righteous shall be saved and the haughty condemned (Isa. 2:4—4:6). The pride of these end time scoffers consists in their **following their own ungodly passions** (cf. vv 11, 16) rather than the rule of faith of the community.

19—The warning applies directly to **these** persons who now create divisions within the Christian community. The combination of **worldly people, devoid of the Spirit, who set up divisions** is reminiscent of a similar problem confronted by Paul at Corinth. There, too, social factions had been created by persons who claimed a superior measure of the Spirit but who, in Paul's assessment, were not spiritual but merely human (see esp. 1 Cor. 2:6-14 and 3:1-4). Jude's response suggests that in his audience also the **scoffers** were making similar false claims about their own spiritual superiority. What they assert, therefore, Jude denies: "They do not have the Spirit" (of God) but are **worldly people** living only for themselves. Purporting to be a spiritual elite, their separatistic (v 12), individualistic (vv 16, 18) and exploitative (v 16) behavior puts the lie to their imperious boasts (v 16).

20-23—The **beloved,** on the other hand, are to counter their contaminating influence by persevering in conduct which fortifies the community. The main clause of vv 20-21, **keep yourselves** (safe from harm) **in the love of God** (cf. v 1), is modified by three participial clauses indicating how this can be accomplished (building yourselves up . . . praying . . . waiting). The building metaphor is widely used in the New Testament for depicting a community of believers constructed through the proclamation of the gospel, established with Jesus Christ as its cornerstone, and maintained through brotherly love (e.g., Rom. 15:20; 1 Cor. 3:10-15; Eph. 2:19-22; 1 Peter 2:5-7). Here in Jude the foundation on which the faithful are to **build themselves up** is their most holy faith, i.e., that faith **once for all delivered to the saints** and now the norm for distinguishing the holy from the unholy.

Second, the beloved are to keep themselves safe by praying in (cf. Eph. 6:18) or "through" (cf. Rom. 8:15-16; Gal. 4:6) **the Holy Spirit,** for they, in contrast to the ungodly (v 19), are the real people of the Spirit. Finally, they are not to give up hope but to keep themselves safe in God's love by waiting for **the mercy of our Lord Jesus Christ** (cf. vv 1, 2) which brings **eternal life** (i.e., the unending life conferred by God on those who do his will; cf. Matt. 25:46; Mark 10:17, 30).

In addition to this triad of participial clauses, these two verses also contain echoes of the trinitarian reference to Holy Spirit, God, and the Lord Jesus Christ (see Matt. 28:19; 1 Cor. 12:4-6; 2 Cor. 13:14: Eph. 4:4-6; 1 Peter 1:2, 3-12) as well as of the traditional triad of faith, hope, and love (see 1 Cor. 13:13; Gal. 5:5-6; Col. 1:4-5; 1 Thess. 1:3; 5:8).

22-23—In conclusion the beloved are counseled regarding their treatment of some community members who, in varying degrees, had already fallen prey to the wiles of the troublemakers. Insulation of the faithful did not yet call for isolation of the victims. The possibility of rescue still remained.

The Greek text here is uncertain. Some manuscripts read only two main clauses, omitting the first **some** of v 23. Other textual witnesses distinguish three groups of backsliders. The latter alternative which is followed by the RSV is supported by Jude's preference for triads. The first group distinguished by this reading of the text, then, involves some believers who had begun to doubt and vascillate in their faith (v 22; see James 1:6-8). These the beloved were to **convince** (according to some manuscripts) or **treat with mercy** (according to other manuscripts), conviction perhaps with reference to the rule of faith (vv 3, 20) and mercy perhaps with reference to the mercy of the Lord (v 21). A second group (v 23a) who were virtually in the **fire** (of destruction, see Matt. 13:42, 50; 25:41) the readers were to **save** by **snatching them out,** as God once rescued his people like a brand plucked from the burning (an image suggested by Amos 4:11; cf. Zech. 3:2). Finally, on **some** (v 23b) who had already been contaminated by the ungodly the beloved were to **have mercy with fear.** Just as clothing is soiled (**spotted**) by contact with unclean bodies, so some believers have been polluted through association with these ungodly persons who defiled their bodies (v 8). Their fate is in the hands of the Holy One. (For the "filthy garment" image see Zech. 3:3-4 and for similar advice regarding the treatment of erring brethren in general see 1 Cor. 5:9-11; 2 Thess. 3:14-15; James 5:19-20.)

24-25—*Concluding Benediction: Praise be to God who will keep you spotless and secure.*

As censorious and negative as its message may be, the letter nevertheless ends on an exultant, positive note. Through an expansive doxology (from *doxa*, "glory," v 25) the beloved are given a final assurance of their divine protection and enduring

sanctification. The benediction combines features that are both
Jewish (the basic doxological form) and Greek (identification
of God as **the only God**, and as **our Savior**, and threefold division of time: **before . . . now . . . for ever**). The benediction is,
therefore, consistent with the mixed style of the letter as a
whole. The use of this liturgical benediction as a conclusion in
place of personal greetings suggests that the letter was composed for public reading during the recipients' gathering for
worship (see also Rom. 16:25-27; 2 Peter 3:18).

In general, the content as well as the form of these verses
closely resembles other Christian doxologies praising God, his
power and other attributes, and the mediatorial role of Jesus
Christ (cf. Rom. 16:25-27; Eph. 3:20-21; 1 Tim. 1:17; 2 Tim.
4:18; Heb. 13:20-21; 1 Peter 4:11; 5:11; 2 Peter 3:18; Martyrdom
of Polycarp 20:2). At the same time, however, the blessing has
been formulated with the situation of the addressees in mind.
Protection **from falling** (a rare term occurring only here in the
New Testament) alludes to the danger to which other erstwhile
believers of the community had already succumbed in their
errant belief and behavior. **To present you without blemish**
derives from an originally cultic expression for the sacrificial
offering of animals "without defect" (and therefore acceptable
to God; see Exod. 29; Lev. 1:3, 10, etc.). The expression, along
with the related term "unspotted," was adopted by early Christians to depict the distinctive holiness and moral purity of the
saints who were sanctified by the blood of the Christ, the
"lamb without blemish or spot" (1 Peter 1:18-19; see also Eph.
1:4; 5:27; Phil. 2:15; Col. 1:22; Heb. 9:14; 2 Peter 3:14). The
beloved are thus assured that it is through God's power that
they can avoid contamination from the defiled (v 8), blemished
(v 12) and spotted (v 23) persons in their midst and thereby
build themselves up on their **most holy faith** (v 20). Preserved
by God in their holiness, they shall surely experience his glorious presence **with** (great) **rejoicing** (see 1 Enoch 103:4; 104:12,
13; Matt. 5:12; 1 Peter 1:6, 8; 4:13).

Finally, the God who **is able** to accomplish this great work of protection and preservation is **our Savior,** the One who once **saved a people** (v 5b) and who now is the Author of **our common salvation** (v 3). **Before all time and now and for ever** is a liturgical prototype for the conclusion of the Gloria Patri which eventually became part of the Christian liturgy.

In this lively combination of denunciation and doxology, excoriation and encouragement, the Letter of Jude has expressed with brief but moving words the earnestness with which fidelity to the faith, Christian unity, and the moral integrity must ever be taken by the followers of Christ. The situation to which it responded was not one that Christians then or later could regard with complacency or disinterest. Given the many repetitions of that scene of deviation and division in subsequent Christian history, the message of Jude is one that the church can ill afford to neglect.

SELECTED BIBLIOGRAPHY

Commentaries and Studies on
1 Peter, 2 Peter, and *Jude*

Dalton, W. J. *Christ's Proclamation to the Spirits:* A Study of
1 Peter 3:18—4:6 (Analecta Biblica 23; Rome: Pontifical Biblical Institute, 1965). A technical study of this passage and
the descent-ascent of Christ in relation to the cosmology of
the times and 1 Enoch in particular.

Danker, F. W. "The Second Letter of Peter," in *Hebrews,
James, 1 and 2 Peter, Jude, Revelation.* Proclamation Commentaries (Philadelphia: Fortress, 1977). A brief, non-tech-
nical overview of 2 Peter and its Hellenistic background.

Elliott, J. H. *A Home for the Homeless.* A Sociological Exegesis
of 1 Peter, Its Situation and Strategy (Philadelphia: Fortress,
1981). A technical interdisciplinary analysis of 1 Peter as a
Christian response to the predicament of social and religious
alienation.

———. *The Elect and the Holy.* An Exegetical Examination of
1 Peter 2:4-10 and the Phrase *Basileion Hierateuma* (Nov-
TSup 12; Leiden: Brill, 1966). A technical study emphasizing the election rather than the priesthood of the Christian
community as the focus of 1 Peter.

———. *1 Peter, Estrangement and Community* (Herald Biblical
Booklets; Chicago: Franciscan Herald Press, 1979). A lay-

oriented introduction to 1 Peter and its "household of God" ecclesiology.

Forneberg, T. *An Early Church in a Pluralistic Society. A Study of 2 Peter* (ConB 9; Lund: Gleerup, 1977). A technical analysis of the dependence of 2 Peter upon Jude and of its cultural setting.

Green, M. *The Second Epistle General of Peter and the General Epistle of Jude* (Tyndale New Testament Commentaries; Grand Rapids: Eerdmans, 1968). A lay-oriented commentary that defends the priority of 2 Peter and its Petrine authorship.

Kelly, J. N. D. *The Epistles of Peter and Jude* (HNTC; New York: Harper, 1969). One of the best and most recent of the commentaries currently available in English on these three books.

Mayor, J. B. *The Epistle of St. Jude and the Second Epistle of St. Peter* (Grand Rapids: Baker, 1965). A reprint of a classic technical study (1907).

Selwyn, E. G. *The First Epistle of St. Peter,* 2nd ed. (London: Macmillan, 1947). The best and most comprehensive commentary on 1 Peter available in English.

Stibbs, A. M. and A. F. Walls. *The First Epistle General of Peter* (Tyndale New Testament Commentaries; Grand Rapids: Eerdmans, 1959). A lay-oriented commentary with an excellent discussion of introductory issues.

Reference Works and Other Pertinent Studies

Barrett, C. K. *The New Testament Background: Selected Documents* (New York: Harper, 1961). An English translation of original sources which illustrate the cultural climate of the New Testament writings, including Epicureanism and Apocalyptic.

Brown, R. E. et al. *Peter in the New Testament:* A Collaborative Assessment by Protestant and Roman Catholic Scholars (Minneapolis: Augsburg, 1973). An ecumenical survey of Peter's significance and role according to the New Testament.

Goppelt, L. *Apostolic and Post-Apostolic Times* (Grand Rapids: Baker, 1977). A reprint of an instructive survey of early Christian history and theology.

Reicke, B. *The New Testament Era.* The World of the Bible from 500 B.C. to A.D. 100 (Philadelphia: Fortress, 1968). The best historical study of the New Testament period currently available in English.

The Interpreter's Dictionary of the Bible. Four Volumes and Supplementary Volume (New York/Nashville: Abingdon, 1962 and 1976). Excellent information by an international team of scholars on all aspects of the Bible, including 1 and 2 Peter and Jude, apocalypticism, pseudepigrapha, and pseudonymous writings.

ABOUT THE AUTHOR

John H. Elliott is a graduate of Concordia Seminary, St. Louis. His Th.D. in New Testament is from the University of Münster, West Germany. Since 1968 he has been professor of theology at the University of San Francisco. Two books, *The Elect and the Holy* (Leiden: E. J. Brill, 1966) and *A Home for the Homeless* (Philadelphia: Fortress, 1981) have established his reputation as a leading authority on 1 Peter.